VICTORY

10 KEYS TO LIVING IN VICTORY EVERY DAY

CAPAZIN THORNTON

VICTORY 10 Keys to Living in Victory Every Day

Copyright © 2014 Capazin Thornton

ALL RIGHTS RESERVED. No portion of this book may be reproduced, stored in a retrieval system, or transmitted in any form or by any means—electronic, mechanical, photocopy, recording, scanning, or other—except for brief quotations in critical reviews or articles, without the prior written permission of the author/publisher.

All Bible quotations, unless otherwise indicated, are taken from the New King James Version®. Copyright © 1982 by Thomas Nelson, Inc. Used by permission. All rights reserved.

Scripture quotations marked (AMP) are taken from the Amplified® Bible. Copyright © 1954, 1958, 1962, 1964, 1965, 1987 by The Lockman Foundation. Used by permission.

VICTORY 10 Keys to Living in Victory Every Day
by Capazin Thornton

ISBN: 978-0-9755473-2-8

Printed in the United States of America

Cover design by Jorgy Jorgensen
Front Cover image © 2014, yevgeniy11 / Fotolia.com

To learn more about and/or request other publications by Capazin Thornton, please visit the website:
http://capazin.com

Dedication

To Christ believers worldwide

to my children Zarie and Jimmy, my daughter-in-law Truly, and grandsons Cameron Mitchel and Morgan, who always inspire me

REVIEWS

VICTORY 10 Keys to Living in Victory Every Day is an easy to understand, straight forward way to live victoriously. Not only is it God's recipe for success, it is also God's desire that everyone live this way. Capazin does a wonderful job of revealing through scripture these keys to victory. A must read.
　—**JAMES L. SMITH, JR** First Vice President – Investment Officer, Wells Fargo Advisors LLC

"Reverence for the Lord" is one key that really touched my heart. While this subject seems to be lost in some of today's recreational churches, Capazin reminds us how vital this key is if we are going to experience victory in our daily lives. Great job!
　—**BISHOP JOSEPH A. McCARGO** President, United Kingdom Network of Churches, Ministries and Businesses

Contents

		Page
	Introduction	1
1	Reverence the Lord	3
2	Word Up	15
3	Renew Your Mind	23
4	Encourage Yourself in the Lord	41
5	Rely on the Person and Power of the Holy Spirit Within	53
6	Consider It Pure Joy	63
7	Rejoice	75
8	Realize You Are Unique, Gifted and Qualified	83
9	Reign Through Heaven's Eyes	93
10	Rise Up, Declare and Decree Victory	107

Introduction

Everybody wants victory in life. We all want healthy relationships, successful endeavors, and to triumph over life's obstacles.

The only problem with victories is that in order to obtain them, we have to go through battles. Unfortunately, many people are not spiritually prepared for the challenging times in which we live. They are good-hearted people, love the Lord, and try to always do the right thing. Yet, they find themselves simply overwhelmed.

If you are one of these people, **VICTORY, 10 Keys to Living in Victory Every Day** was written for you. Born out of my own struggles to press through to victory and not be a victim of tough times and tough people, I am confident that you are at the right place and right time for your breakthrough.

You are holding 10 powerful keys that will revolutionize your life. Each key is based on Bible revelation and will provide illumination, encouragement, strength, and practical know-how to help you blast through oppressive situations, overcome obstacles, and prevail.

Read this book. Meditate on it. Get these principles into your spirit. I hope that **VICTORY 10 Keys to Living in Victory Every Day** will become one of your favorite resources for inspiration, encouragement and empowerment.

I pray that God's wisdom will abound to you. I pray that God will flood your spirit with His marvelous light and that you will hear His voice within these pages. I pray that God will give you the precise word you need for your breakthrough, so that no matter what you face, you will know how to lay hold to victory.

May God's amazing peace, love, and grace be multiplied to you today and every day.

Capazin Thornton

Key No. 1:

Reverence the Lord

> The fear of the Lord is the beginning of knowledge, but fools despise wisdom and instruction. ~ Prov 1:7

Reverence for the Lord is the key that opens the door to one possessing true knowledge, perception, skill, understanding, intelligence, wisdom, and discernment.

To reverence the Lord means to *honor, fear* and *respect* Him. It means to *worship* and *stand in awe of Him*, to love, obey and be devoted to Him, and to walk in humility before Him.

The psalmist declares:

Holy and reverend is His name ~ Ps 111:19b

Let all the earth fear the Lord [revere and worship Him]; let all the inhabitants of the world stand in awe of Him. ~ Ps 33:8 (AMP)

When one fails to show respect for God

Having and showing respect for God would seem a no-brainer. However, consider Hosea 4:6. God says, "My people are destroyed for lack of knowledge."

The word translated destroyed means *to be dumb or silent*; hence *to fail or perish*. Some of God's people act in dumb ways, suffer failures, and even perish because they fail to show respect for God.

Samson

Samson anointed judge-deliverer

After the death of Joshua, judges ruled Israel for about three hundred thirty-years. The judges were civil, military and spiritual leaders (judge-deliverers). God appointed Samson to be a judge-deliverer and anointed him with supernatural strength to lead Israel in its fight against the Philistines.

Samson's Achilles heel

Samson judged Israel for twenty years. At some point along the way he became captivated by the enemy's women. Ultimately his love for Philistine women became his Achilles heel. Samson was easy prey for Delilah whom the Philistine lords promised to pay a *truckload* of silver to find out the secret of Samson's great strength. (Judges 15:20-16:5)

Samson loved Delilah. But Delilah was on a mission for the money. She betrayed Samson on three occasions when she thought he had revealed the secret of his great strength.

Delilah nagged Samson every single day to tell her his secret. Finally Samson caved in and told Delilah that the secret of his strength was his uncut hair (which was the symbol of his covenant with God). So, while Samson slept, Delilah had all his hair shaved off. She then gave him into the hands of the Philistines.

Samson lost his vision and anointing

Samson thought he could break away as before. "But he did not know that the Lord had departed from him" (Judges 16:20). Samson's sensitivity to the Spirit of God had completely dulled.

After the Philistines captured him, they put out his eyes. It certainly was sad that Samson lost his natural eyesight. It was even sadder that he lost his spiritual vision, perception, and anointing.

Samson's revenge cost him his life

Samson asked the Lord to give him supernatural strength just one more time so he could take revenge on the Philistines. The Lord granted his request.

Samson killed the most Philistines ever when he uprooted the pillars of their temple and caused it to collapse on them. Tragically, Samson died with them. Ultimately it can be said that Samson's demise was because he lost his reverence and awe for the Lord.

King Solomon

Solomon the wise

In 1 Kings Chapter 3, the Lord appeared to Solomon in a dream and invited him to ask for anything he wanted. Solomon asked God to give him wisdom so that he would know how to judge God's people.

God was pleased with Solomon's request. It showed his humility, his utmost respect for God, and that he cared for God's people.

God gave Solomon a wise and understanding heart like no other. He also gave him riches and honor that far surpassed all the kings of the earth.

King Solomon became famous for his remarkable wisdom, immense wealth, and expansive building projects. He built the first temple for God in Jerusalem.

Solomon's mind was so keen that he knew 3,000 proverbs and wrote 1,005 songs. Solomon the wise was so great that only when Jesus of Nazareth arrived on the scene was one described as *greater*. (1 Ki 4:32; Mt 12:42)

Solomon the foolish

Yet in his later years, King Solomon became very

forgetful and foolish. Among other things, he forgot God's law which forbade Israelites to marry women from the nations they dispossessed. The law also forbade a king to have multiple wives. Solomon had 700 foreign princess wives and 300 mistresses. (Deut 7:3-4; 17:17; 1 Ki 11:1-3)

These pagan women influenced the King to worship idols. "For it was so, when Solomon was old, that his wives turned his heart after other gods, and his heart was not loyal to the Lord his God, as was the heart of his father David" (1 Ki 11:4). King Solomon even built temples for his foreign wives to burn incense and sacrifice to their idols.

Judgment for Solomon's sins fell upon succeeding generations. After Solomon's death, the kingdom of Israel was divided. A few hundred years later, the Babylonians destroyed Jerusalem and Solomon's temple and kept the Jews in captivity seventy years. (1 Ki 11:9-13)

God had appeared to Solomon not once, but twice. Even so, Solomon turned away from God and fell into idolatry. He also damaged his legacy as a great leader of God's people. All because he failed to continue to fear, revere, honor, and respect God.

In the end Solomon got it right

Near the end of his life, Solomon got it right when he summed up the duty of mankind as: "... fear [honor] God and obey His commands ... " (Eccl 12:13).

When people show respect for God

The Hebrew midwives

The Hebrew midwives Siphrah and Puah lived in Moses' day. The king of Egypt had instructed the midwives to kill all the male Hebrew babies while they were being birthed.

The midwives refused to carry out this hideous order. They deliberately saved the male infants alive. When brought before the king they told him that the male babies were lively and delivered quickly before the midwives arrived.

The Hebrew midwives feared God. Because they feared God and not man, God blessed these midwives with households of their own. (Ex 1:15-21)

Peter and John

The apostles Peter and John were thrown in jail for preaching and healing in the Name of Jesus. The religious leaders later released them with a stern warning not to speak or teach any more in that name. Peter and the other apostles replied, "We must obey God rather than man" (Acts 5:29).

Not intimidated by the threats of men, Peter and John chose to honor, respect, and obey the One who saved, anointed, commissioned and privileged them to preach, teach, and heal in His name.

As the result, God used Peter and John mightily to build His kingdom and spread the gospel. Their legacy as ministers of God continues to live through the books of the Bible that bear their names.

God's promises to those who reverence Him

God promises great blessings to those who reverence Him. Here are ten fantastic promises:

1. The Lord takes pleasure

> ...The Lord takes pleasure in those who fear Him.... ~ Ps 147:11

The Lord takes pleasure in Cornelius

Cornelius was a first century Roman soldier. The Bible says, "He was a devout, God-fearing man, as was everyone in his household. He gave generously to the poor and prayed regularly to God" (Acts 10:2, NLT).

Cornelius was a Gentile. He was outside of the covenants and promises God made with Israel. Yet Cornelius captured God's attention because he wholeheartedly reverenced, prayed to and worshiped Israel's God.

Besides personally reverencing and worshipping God, Cornelius led his household to do the same. Consequently, God sent the apostle Peter to Cornelius' house to preach the good news of salvation through Jesus Christ. All who heard believed and were filled with the Holy Spirit. (Acts 10)

The Lord takes pleasure in those who reverence Him.

2. God will reveal divine secrets to you

> The secret of the Lord is with those who fear Him, and He will show them His covenant. ~ Ps 25:14

When you have a holy respect for the Lord, He will reveal divine secrets (treasures of wisdom and knowledge) and give you a deeper understanding of His covenant with you.

3. God will give you wealth and riches

> Wealth and riches *will be* in his house and his righteousness endures forever. ~ Ps 112:3

> By humility and the fear of the Lord are riches and honor and life. ~ Prov 22:4

God will see to it that wealth and riches, substance, sufficiency, and well-being are in your house.

You will be blessed financially. Your soul will be at peace. Because you honor God, He will honor you. All will be well with you, and your whole household will be blessed.

4. God will fulfill your heart's desire

> He will fulfill the desire of those who fear Him . . . ~ Ps 145:19a

God is *essentially, absolutely and consummately good*. When you reverence Him, He will fulfill the righteous desires of your heart.

5. God will hear your cry, rescue and deliver you

> . . . He also will hear their cry and save them. ~ Ps 145:19b

When you call out for help, God will hear your cry, rescue and deliver you.

6. The angel of the Lord encamps around you

> The angel of the Lord encamps all around those who fear Him, and delivers them. ~ Ps 34:7

When you reverence the Lord, the angel of the Lord encamps (pitches his tent) around you. He will defend and protect you.

I am reminded when the Assyrian king Sennacherib laid siege to Judah and boasted that no god could deliver Judah out of his hand, God sent one angel who wiped out 185,000 Assyrian soldiers (2 Ki 19:35). Wow! One angel is all you need to encamp around, defend and protect you.

7. Your descendants will be mighty

> His descendants will be mighty on the

earth; the generation of the upright will be blessed. ~ Ps 112:2

The descendants of those who reverence God will be mighty on the earth. While your descendants will have to personally choose whether to receive God's gift of salvation, they are blessed in advance when their godly forbearers pray for them and pass to them knowledge of and reverence for the Lord.

8. God's exceedingly great mercy is over your life

> For as the heavens are high above the earth, so great is His mercy toward those who fear Him. ~ Ps 103:11

When you reverence God, His exceedingly great mercy is over your life.

9. You will not be afraid

> He will not be afraid of evil tidings; his heart is steadfast, trusting in the Lord. His heart is established; he will not be afraid... ~ Ps 112:7, 8a

When you fear and trust God, you will not be afraid of any bad news or evil reports.

10. You are blessed

> Praise the LORD! Blessed is the man who fears the LORD, who delights greatly in His

commandments. ~ Ps 112:1

When you fear God, you are blessed, literally, *oh so happy, happy.* Blessedness is the state of well-being, lightheartedness, gladness of heart, and optimism that comes when you delight in God and His Word. In this blessed state you are free to fulfill your highest potential.

Recapture the awe and reverence

Is it possible to recapture the awe and reverence we had for the Lord when we first believed? Absolutely! Let us ask God to do a fresh work in our heart.

> Father, I admit that at times I have failed to give you reverence. Forgive me for not taking a stand when others around me said and did things that clearly showed a lack of respect and honor towards you. Forgive me for choosing favor of men over pleasing God. I repent from blasé attitudes, indifference, negative thinking, speaking, and acting. Create in me a clean heart and renew a steadfast spirit within me. Unite my heart to fear your Name.
>
> Father, I love you. From this day forward I purpose to give you first place in my life and to honor, respect, and reverence you in thought, word, and deed. Thank you

for performing a fresh work in me. In Jesus' Name, I pray. Amen.

[Scripture Refs: Ps 51:10; Ps 86:11]

Look to the future with confident expectation

When you reverence the Lord, you can look to the future with confident expectation. You will not be shaken by bad news nor will you live in dread of the future. You can be confident that Almighty God has you covered from top to bottom, front to back, beginning to end.

By purposing in your heart to always honor, respect, and reverence the Lord, you have taken the first step to living each day on a strong note of victory.

> Therefore, since we are receiving a kingdom which cannot be shaken, let us have grace, by which we may serve God acceptably with reverence and godly fear. ~ Heb. 12:28

Key No. 2:

Word Up

> For the Word that God speaks is alive and full of power [making it active, operative, energizing, and effective] . . . ~ Heb 4:12 (AMP)

Knowing, applying, speaking and acting on God's Word is foundational to living in victory every day. It is the key to becoming established in truth.

No matter what seemingly insurmountable challenge you face, you can Word up, lay hold to God's promises, break through the obstacles, stand your ground, and prevail.

God's Word is alive and powerful

God's Word is alive and powerful (divinely explosive). Inherent in God's Word is supernatural, miraculous, life giving, situation changing power!

While there are many books that can stimulate our minds and creative imaginations and inspire and motivate us, there is only one book in the universe that has the power to raise the dead, open blind eyes, cause demons to flee, transform a sinner's heart, and heal, deliver and restore broken, bruised and crushed people. That book is the Bible, the written Word of God, the revealed will of God.

The Bible reveals absolute truth, that is, truth from the divine perspective. It provides the keys to living an abundant, God-favored, victorious life.

Smith Wigglesworth said:

> Never think or never say that this Book contains the Word of God. It is the Word of God. It is supernatural in origin, eternal in duration, inexpressible in value, infinite in scope, regenerative in power, infallible in authority, universal in interest, personal in application, inspired in totality. Read it through. Write it down. Pray it in. Work it out. And then pass it on. (*Faith that Prevails*, pp. 15-16)

The apostle Peter says that the Word of God is *incorruptible seed which lives and abides forever* (1 Pet 1:23).

God's Promise Book

The Bible is a book of revelation, vision, encouragement and hope. Also called the *Word of God, Holy Scriptures, Word of Truth, Word of Life, Word of Faith*, the Bible is God's promise book. It is filled with God's exceedingly great and precious promises.

The New Covenant was ratified by Christ's blood. It is through Jesus Christ that we can have relationship with God and access the promises of God.

The Bible says that all the promises of God in Christ are "*Yes*" and "Amen" (2 Cor 1:20). In Christ God's promises (Old and New Testament) are true, faithful, and certain. This clearly lets us know that no promise of God was ever intended to be unobtainable.

Here are a few of God's promises regarding commonly faced challenges.

Famine (hunger, scarcity, lack)?

The Lord is my Shepherd, I shall not lack. ~ Ps 23:1

And God is able to make all grace abound toward you; that you, always having all sufficiency in all things, may abound to every good work. ~ 2 Cor 9:8

Feeling weak?

Finally, my brethren, be strong in the Lord

and in the power of His might. ~ Eph 6:10

Fearful?

For God has not given us a spirit of fear, but of power and of love and of a sound mind. ~ 2 Tim 1:7

Family problems?

So they said, "Believe on the Lord Jesus Christ, and you will be saved, you and your household." ~ Acts 16:31

The wicked are overthrown and are no more, but the house of the righteous will stand [endure]. ~ Prov 12:7

Feeling heavy or burdened?

Put on ". . . the garment of praise for the spirit of heaviness . . ." ~ Isa 61:3

Rejoice in the Lord always. Again I will say, rejoice! ~ Phil 4:4

In His presence is fullness of joy. ~ Ps 16:11

Feeling unsure of what to do next?

Trust in the Lord with all your heart, and lean not on your own understanding; in all your ways acknowledge Him, and He shall direct your paths. ~ Prov 3:5-6

The unfolding of your words gives light;

it gives understanding to the simple. ~ Ps 119:130, NASB

However, when He, the Spirit of truth, has come, He will guide you into all truth . . . He will tell you things to come. ~ Jn 16:13

God wants us to lay hold to His promises by faith. Through faith and perseverance we will inherit the promises. (Heb 6:12)

Keys for Success

The Bible is the greatest success book ever written! If we truly want success in life, we must make knowing God's Word a priority.

1. Read the whole Bible

The first step to *Word up* then is to find out what the Bible says in its entirety. If you have never read the whole Bible, now is a good time to start. You might say, "I don't have time to read the whole Bible." Oh, really? Check this out:

> The Bible is comprised of 66 books, 1189 chapters. You could sit down and read it through in less than 60 hours.
>
> If you read 3 chapters a day + 5 on Sunday, you could read it through in 12 months.
>
> If you read 40 chapters a day, you will read the entire Bible in 30 days.

If you read one chapter a day in the New Testament, you will finish the New Testament in 30 days.

Choose a reading plan that works for you and start reading the *Book of Life*.

2. Pay attention to God's Word

> My son, give attention to my words; incline your ear to my sayings. ~ Prov 4:20

God tells us to give attention to His words. To give attention means *to hear, be attentive, heed, pay attention, listen.*

God says to *incline* our *ears* to his sayings. To incline means to *stretch out towards*, to *prick up*. Have you ever noticed when a dog hears a siren or loud sound how his ears prick straight up? In like manner, our ears should prick up every time we hear God's Word. Our ears should stretch out to listen to what God is saying.

3. Do not let God's words out of your sight

> Do not let them depart from your eyes; keep them in the midst of your heart. ~ Prov 4:21

God tells us to keep His words before our eyes. We should always be reading the Word. We should memorize Scripture. We should treasure and keep God's words in our heart.

4. Search the Scriptures

> For, they are life to those who find them,
> and health to all their flesh. ~ Prov 4:22

God's words are life to those who find them—to those who search for and lay hold to them. In addition to your reading plan, make a habit of searching the Scriptures to find God's answers and promises for every area of your life.

Also, after you have heard God's Word preached or taught, follow up by searching the Scriptures to be sure what you heard lines up with what is actually written.

5. Guard your heart

> Keep your heart with all diligence, for out
> of it spring the issues of life. ~ Prov 4:23

To keep your heart with all diligence is to guard, preserve and protect it. The heart speaks of your inner man, your spirit, your innermost self. Out of your heart springs *issues, forces, exits, escape ways, deliverance.*

God's Word provides the exits, escape ways, and deliverance for the challenges we face. When we fill our hearts with God's Word, then the Holy Spirit can bring to mind the precise Word we need to lay hold to, stand on, and speak forth in any situation.

6. Speak, meditate, and observe to do God's Word

> This Book of the Law shall not depart from your mouth, but you shall meditate in it day and night, that you may observe to do according to all that is written in it. For then you will make your way prosperous, and then you will have good success. ~ Josh 1:8

From these instructions given to Joshua, we can learn three important keys to *Word up*:

Speak God's Word. The key to releasing the power of Scripture is to speak it out with boldness, faith, and expectation.

Meditate in God's Word. Think on, contemplate, ponder, study, utter, and recite the Word day and night.

Always observe to do the Word. When you read a passage of Scripture, ask yourself, "What does this Scripture require me to do?" Write it down. Then, do it.

7. Make your way prosperous

The result is you will make your way (course of life, journey) prosperous and you will have good success. In other words, keep reading, believing, speaking, and doing what the Word says and you will *push forward*, *break out*, and *deal wisely* in every area of your life.

Key No. 3:

Renew Your Mind

> And do not be conformed to this world, but be transformed by the renewing of your mind, that you may prove what is that good and acceptable and perfect will of God. ~ Rom 12:2

To renew your mind is crucial to living in victory every day. Renew means to *renovate, repair, recondition, reconstitute, revive, rejuvenate, refresh, resurrect*. Renewing your mind is the key to thinking and acting like God originally intended—full of God-inspired thoughts, creative ideas, sparkling life, and purpose.

Original Man: created in the image of God

> So God created man in His own image; in the image of God He created him; male and female He created them. ~ Gen 1:27

God created humans in His image and likeness, to bear a similitude in appearance or quality to God. He made us each an eternal spirit, with a soul (mind, will, emotions, personality), in a physical body.

God created us with spiritual, moral, intellectual, rational, and emotional attributes. The mind is the seat of our creative imagination, intellect, abstract reasoning, memory, reflection, thoughts, and understanding.

The original man Adam had an awesome mind. The Bible says Adam named all the living creatures God made. (Gen 2:19) Wow!

Fallen Man: darkened, distorted, perverted soul

Adam sinned against God and ushered in sin and death upon all humanity. Death is not a cessation of life. It is a separation:

- Our spirits became separated from the life of God.
- Our souls became darkened, distorted, perverted, and separated from the life of the spirit.

- Our bodies succumbed to decay, sickness and disease and ultimately physical death (a separation of the body from the spirit and soul).

[*See* Rom 5:12; Gen 2:17; 3:6; 3:7; 3:9; 3:19]

Total Salvation: experienced in three stages

Christ came to save us and restore us to right relationship with God. Through His death on the cross, Christ paid the price in full for our total salvation—spirit, soul, and body. Salvation, however, is experienced in three stages:

- Instant spiritual rebirth and re-connection to the life of God
- Progressive restoration of our soul (mind, will, emotions, personality)
- Future body transformation

The moment we receive Christ, the Holy Spirit regenerates our spirit. We are spiritually reborn in an instant.

Our soul (mind, will, emotions, and personality) is restored day by day over the course of our lives to the degree we renew our mind on God's Word and cooperate with the Holy Spirit's work within us.

Our body will be transformed into a glorious immortal body when Christ returns. In the meantime, because Christ paid the price for our healing, we can receive healing and walk in health now.

[Scripture refs: Ps 23:31; Rom 12:1-2; Jas 1:21; 1 Cor 15:51-54; 1 Thess 5:23]

The need to renew our mind

Our fragmented soul must be made whole

When born again we receive a new spirit, but keep the same old soul. That old soul is perverted and fragmented because of sin and having been programmed all our life with wrong thoughts, concepts, feelings, intentions, and desires based on negative life experiences and failures, as well as wrong ideologies, philosophies, opinions, theories, surmising, superstition, half-truths and out-and-out lies.

God's Word has the power to renew, renovate, repair, recondition, reconstitute, revive, rejuvenate, refresh, and restore our entire soul. Through God's great and precious promises, we can partake of His divine nature and in the process of time be radically transformed. (2 Pet 1:4)

A war continually rages against our minds

A war continually rages against our minds from two realms, one visible and the other invisible.

The visible realm

The world in which we live, the visible realm, is full of people who do not know God. God loves them. But they are unregenerate, separated from the life of

God and blinded to the light and truth of God's Word, just as we once were. (1 Cor 2:14; 2 Cor 4:4)

For the most part, unregenerate people live independent of and with little regard for God. They are ruled by the *lust of the flesh*, the *lust of the eyes*, and the *pride of life*. (1 Jn 2:16) They are under the sway of the devil and his evil empire which operate from the invisible realm.

The invisible realm

The Bible reveals there are three regions called heaven. The highest heaven (*the third heaven*) is the abode of God, His angelic host, and the spirits of the righteous made perfect. This region is invisible to us. However, if God so chooses He can open our spiritual eyes to allow us a glimpse of things in heaven. (2 Cor 12:2; Heb 9:24; Heb 12:23)

The second heaven is the stellar heaven, the expanse above the earth containing the sun, moon, stars and planets. (Isa 13:10) The first heaven is the lower atmospheric heaven surrounding the earth. (Jer 4:25)

The devil and his host of evil spirits operate in the invisible realm of the first and second heavens. They work to try to dominate people and policies in the visible realm.

***

For point of illustration, you may have seen the *fantasy* movie, "The Lord of the Rings: The Fellowship of the Ring." In the story, Frodo Baggins is the inheritor of a magical ring called the One Ring. Frodo finds out the One Ring is malevolent, created by a dark lord whose goal is dominion over the free people of Middle-earth.

Frodo and companions (the fellowship of the ring) journey through treacherous lands headed to a volcanic mountain called Mount Doom. Mount Doom is the place where the ring was originally forged and the only place where it can be destroyed.

The ring has supernatural power including the power to make the wearer of the ring invisible. When Frodo needed a quick escape, he put the ring on. He quickly disappeared from the visible realm. But then he found himself in the invisible realm where he could see the evil spirits who were trying to kill him and regain the ring for their dark lord.

***

Satan is the dark lord in the invisible realm surrounding the earth. Called the *god of this world* and the *prince of the power of the air,* the devil and his evil forces work nonstop to undermine, contradict and discredit God. The devil will use whoever he can and whatever means he can to accomplish this goal. (2 Cor 4:4; Eph 2:2; Eph 6:12)

Is it any wonder that the media is filled with perversion, extreme violence, obsession with death and demons, all sorts of trivia, trashy ideas, lying vanities, and nonsensical things that contradict God's Word?

In order to walk in victory, we must break the power of these evil influences. We must make sure our inner man is strong. And, we must know how to deal with the thoughts that come our way.

Be ready for spiritual battles

We need supernatural armor and weaponry in order to be ready for spiritual battles and to stand victorious against supernatural foes. God has provided the precise armor and weaponry we need to be victorious. (Eph 6:10-18)

Put on, take up, and release the power of the whole armor of God

The Word commands us to *put on* the *whole armor of God*. To put on means "to sink into (clothing)." We sink into the armor when we declare it. The armor God provides is supernatural with divinely explosive miraculous power.

Defensively, the whole armor will protect and fortify our inner man and give us the ability to stand our ground and withstand any spiritual attacks.

Offensively, when we pray and declare God's Word of truth, His righteousness, His peace, His salvation, and faith in God through Christ, the armor works to become a powerful *super weapon*.

When we hurl bold faith declarations, exuberant praise and heartfelt prayer into the atmospheric heaven, the forces of darkness are scattered. Breakthroughs come.

Let's release this *super weapon* right now in faith:

Belt of Truth

Heavenly Father, thank you for the powerful spiritual armor you provide. Thank you for truth. Your Word is truth. Jesus is the way, the truth and the life. The Holy Spirit is the eternal Spirit of Truth, who shows me the way into all truth. Lead me in your path of light and truth today.

Father, I purpose to let truth settle and abide in my heart. I purpose to walk in integrity of heart. I will think, speak, and operate in truth and truthfulness. Thank you, Lord, for the freedom that comes from knowing Christ and living according to the truth of your holy Word.

Breastplate of Righteousness

Thank you, Father, for imputing Christ's righteousness to me. I am the righteousness of God through faith in Christ Jesus. Thank you that I have a position of right standing with you and am seated in heavenly places in Christ. I declare that your kingdom of righteousness, peace, and joy in the Holy Spirit rules and reigns in me and over my life.

Gospel Shoes of Peace

Father, I thank you for the good news that

Christ made peace with you for me through the blood of his cross. As the result, I now have double peace—peace with God and the supernatural peace of God which surpasses all understanding. God's peace guards my mind and rules my heart. I will not be moved by outer disturbances. I stand with confidence in the safety, security, tranquility, good success, prosperity, comfort and peace I have in Christ. In Him I live, move, and have my being. Thank you, Father, for keeping me in perfect peace as I keep my mind stayed on you.

Shield of Faith

Father, I hold out above all the shield of faith which extinguishes all the fiery missiles of the wicked one. I fight the good fight of faith. I give no place to doubt, fear or unbelief. I walk by faith and not by sight. My faith is totally in you and your Word. I trust you completely with my life. I will not lean to my own understanding. I acknowledge you in all my ways and confidently expect you to direct my path.

Helmet of salvation

Thank you, Father, for the helmet of salvation that protects my mind. Thank you for the total salvation you have provided for me in by and through Christ Jesus. Thank you for eternal life and the blessed hope that one day I will have a glorified body. Thank you for forgiving my sins, healing my body, daily protecting and delivering me. Thank you Lord that as I renew my mind on your word, you restore my soul. Thank you for preserving me spirit, soul, and body.

Sword of the Spirit

Father, I thank you for your Word which is alive, powerful, energizing, effective, and sharper than any two-edged sword. Father, may the Holy Spirit give me the precise Word I need for every situation I encounter today. By your Word I will cast down every image, argument and reasoning that tries to exalt itself against the knowledge of Christ. I will bring your Word to bear in every situation.

Lord, thank you for the whole spiritual armor whereby I stand confidently and victoriously against all the schemes and strategies of the devil. In the mighty Name of Jesus Christ, my Lord, I pray. Amen.

[Scripture Refs: *Truth*—Jn 17:17; 14:6; 14:17; 16:13; *Righteousness*—2 Cor 5:21; 1 Cor 1:30; Eph 2:6; Rom 14:17; *Peace*—Col 1:20; Eph 2:14; Rom 5:1; Phil 4:6-7; Isa 55:12; Acts 17:28; Isa 26:3; *Faith*—Eph 6:17; 1 Tim 6:12; 2 Cor 5:7; Mk 11:22; Prov 3:5; *Salvation*—Rom 10:9-10; 8:16; 1:16; Gal 3:13; Ps 23:3; 1 Thess 5:23; *Word*—Heb 4:12; 2 Cor 10:5; Rom 8:1; Eph 6:11]

How to deal with thoughts

How do we deal with thoughts that come our way? First, let us understand that thoughts, good or bad, come to life only if we choose to receive them, believe them, and act on them. Here is a simple formula of how thoughts (good or bad) come to life:

A thought + human will = conception

How we handle the thoughts that come our way will determine whether we walk in victory or suffer defeat.

Consider this famous quote by Ralph Waldo Emerson:

> Sow a thought and you reap an action.
> Sow an act and you reap a habit.
> Sow a habit and you reap a character.
> Sow a character and you reap a destiny.

In other words, what we think on (good or bad) will affect our actions, habits, character, and destiny.

Discern the source

We have to discern the source of every thought we allow our minds to linger on. Is it from (1) **God**, (2) **us**, (3) **other people**, or (4) the **devil**?

Thoughts within

A thought is a mental image, concept, idea, notion or purpose. Thoughts within can come from our **conscience**, from **the Holy Spirit** who speaks within our spirit, or from **our soul** (mind, will, emotions). Thoughts springing from our soul are many times influenced by thoughts from without.

Thoughts from without

Thoughts from without can come to us through people, the media, and demonic spirits. A thought can be lodged in our minds from a simple whisper in the ear, from pictures flashed before our eyes, from things we read, from words spoken to us, things we hear, music we listen to. In other words, from sense organ stimuli—what we see, hear, smell, taste, and touch.

Filter thoughts

It is crucial that we filter what we listen to and watch. Most definitely we have to stop listening to opinions coming from unregenerate, carnal people who do not know God. These people's minds are corrupted by sin. They are under the sway of the devil.

We should not give audience to any voice that contradicts God's Word and His character. To do so is to invite confusion. If we meditate on confusion, we will undoubtedly bring distraction to our minds, disturb our peace, and spiritually disarm ourselves.

Take authority over and cast down ungodly thoughts

Take authority over and cast down ungodly thoughts. An ungodly thought is any thought that opposes the clear revelation of Scripture.

Do not think on or say things that contradict God's Word no matter how popular or trendy they may be in our culture. We cannot afford to latch onto catchy phrases just because we hear people all around us saying them.

Do not let the fears, opinions, and darkened world view of people who do not know God cast a shadow on your faith in God, His excellence, and His boundless supply. Cast down any thought, image, argument, reasoning, logic, rationale that contradicts God's Word.

Hold your thoughts and words up to God's checklist

> Finally, brethren, whatever things are true, whatever things are noble, whatever things are just, whatever things are pure, whatever things are lovely, whatever things are of good report, if there is any virtue and if there is anything praiseworthy—meditate on these things. ~Phil 4:8

Philippians 4:8 provides a checklist of characteristics for right thinking, which applies equally to right speaking:

1. True — accurate, genuine [not assumptions, half-truths or hearsay]
2. Noble — Honorable, thoughts befitting kings and queens
3. Just — Right

4.	Pure	Clean, uncontaminated, clear
5.	Lovely	Friendly towards, delightful
6.	A good report	Pleasant [never bad reports, gossips, rumors]
7.	Virtuous	Excellent, having great moral value
8.	Praiseworthy	Worthy of praise, thoughts that glorify God

Remember, this is a checklist, not a smorgasbord. We do not get to pick and choose one or two favorite characteristics while ignoring the rest. Go through the whole list point by point to see if what you think about (and say) passes all eight characteristics.

Think on God's goodness, love, and grace

Don Moen wrote a beautiful melodic song, which words are these:

"Think about His love

Think about His goodness

Think about His grace that's brought us through

For as high as the heavens above

So great is the measure of our Father's love

Great is the measure of our Father's love."

This is a simple yet powerful song that focuses on God's goodness, love and grace—things that are indeed true, noble, just, pure, lovely, a good report, virtuous, and praiseworthy, things on which we can renew our minds.

Set your mind on things above

> If then you were raised with Christ, seek those things which are above, where Christ is, sitting at the right hand of God. Set your mind on things above, not on things on the earth. ~ Col 3:1-2

Adopt the mind of Christ

We must adopt the mind of Christ. The Bible tells us we have the mind of Christ.

The *mind of Christ* is spiritual, not intellectual. It means having thoughts, feelings, will, purpose, ways and attitudes like Christ. For instance, while in the earth, Jesus' self-description was "I am gentle and humble."

Certainly it is paramount for Christ believers to know who we are, what we have, and what we can do in Christ. It is equally important to develop character and possess the mind of Christ.

We must be humble (*I am what I am by the grace of God*) and gentle (*wise as serpents and harmless as doves*). (1 Cor 2:16, 15:10; Mt 11:29; see Phil 2:5-8)

Renew your mind every day on God's Word

Read, study, recite, and listen to God's Word as often each day as you can. God's Word is spiritual food that will sustain and strengthen you. The more of God's Word you retain and apply to your life, the stronger you will become. God's Word will enable you to cheerfully persevere through all of life's battles.

Break the power of negative thoughts and words

When God's Word is spoken over people and situations where negative words have ruled and reigned, God's Word will dethrone them. God's Word will render them powerless, null and void.

Where negative words brought sickness and disease, God's Word will bring healing! Where negative words brought poverty and lack, God's Word will bring abundance! Where negative words brought fear, God's Word will bring perfect love and peace!

God's Word carries life and will destroy the power of negative words that carry the law of sin and death. To destroy means *to ruin the structure*. It also means *to deprive of position, prestige, and reputation and of the power to oppose or offer resistance.*

Let's make a prayer declaration together to break the power of negative thoughts and words off our lives.

> Father, I thank you for your light and truth. Thank you for reminding me of how important it is to censor what I watch, listen to, think about, and say. I realize that I have given the devil access into my life through

the gates of my eyes, ears, and mouth. I have listened to, watched, and said things I shouldn't have. Forgive me.

Right now, in the Name of Jesus, I take authority over and break the power of evil thoughts breathed out to me through the media. I take authority over and break the power of ungodly words and sight pictures projected to my mind. I take authority over and break the power of evil reports and curses spoken to me, about me, over me, against me, over my family and household. I declare the blood of Jesus covers me, my mind, my body, my soul, my spirit.

From this day forward, I purpose to filter what I watch and listen to. I will not counsel with ungodly people. I will not allow the influence of ungodly people to come into my life through various media.

From now on, Philippians 4:8 is my thought checklist. I will cast down images, arguments, and reasoning that oppose God and His Word. I will replace corrupt, unholy thoughts with the high thoughts of God revealed in the Bible.

I declare that I have a sound mind and I will make right decisions and sound choices. I have the mind of Christ and hold his thoughts, attitudes, feelings and purposes in my heart.

I will meditate on things that are true, noble, just, pure, lovely, of good report, virtuous, and praiseworthy. I will set my mind on things above. I will be transformed by daily renewing my mind on the Word of God. In the Name of Jesus! Amen.

[Scripture refs: Lk 10:19; 2 Tim 1:7; 1 Cor 2:16; Phil 4:8; Col 3:2]

Expect a dynamic change

As we renew our minds every day on God's Word and develop a habit of thinking only on things that pass God's thought checklist, changes begin to take place in our lives. Focus, clarity, strength, and soundness of mind come. Before long, our entire way of thinking, communicating, and acting changes to the positive. More and more we find ourselves becoming like people re-created in the image of God.

Key No. 4:

Encourage Yourself in the Lord

> . . . David encouraged and strengthened himself in the Lord his God. ~ 1 Sam 30:6b (AMP)

Every adverse situation you face provides the greatest opportunity to encourage and strengthen yourself in the Lord.

President John F. Kennedy said, "When written in Chinese, the word 'crisis' is composed of two characters. One represents danger and the other represents opportunity." The fact is, no matter what crisis, trouble, or difficulty you face, you have an excellent opportunity to encourage and strengthen yourself in the Lord. This is the key to experiencing God's faithfulness.

King David's crisis

King David was no stranger to adversity or crisis. When he was a lad, he pursued and killed a lion and a bear which took one of his father's lambs. Later, he faced the giant Goliath and killed him with a slingshot and smooth stone.

Then the anointed harpist, who once soothed King Saul's anguished soul, became the object of Saul's intense jealousy, rage, and treachery. David stayed on the run from Saul ten or more years, often living from hand to mouth, in caves and strongholds in the mountains, forest, and desert.

In 1 Samuel 30, the soon-to-be king of Israel is facing yet another crisis. While David and his men left their families in Ziklag to pursue military campaigns, the Amalekites invaded Ziklag, took spoils, set the city on fire, and carried away the wives and children of David and his men. The Amalekites no doubt were retaliating for David's previous raids on them. (1 Sam 27:8-9).

You may recall the Amalekites had the audacity to attack the faint and weary rear ranks of the children of Israel during their exodus from Egypt.

Certainly the Amalekites heard about the great God who delivered the children of Israel out of Egypt with mighty signs and wonders. Yet, they showed no fear of Him when they attacked His people. So God promised to blot out the remembrance of Amalek from under heaven. (Deut 25:17-19)

In 1 Samuel 15, God commanded King Saul to utterly destroy the Amalekites along with all their possessions. Saul disobeyed, sparing the best of the sheep and oxen and Agag the king (although Samuel later executed Agag). Also, some of the Amalekites may have escaped along with the Kenites before the battle with Saul. If all the Amalekites had been destroyed, there would not have been an Amalekite around to invade Ziklag. Ultimately, an Amalekite would claim to have killed the critically wounded Saul. (1 Sam 15:6; 2 Sam 1:5-10)

Now, when David and his men returned to Ziklag, they found the city up in smoke and their wives and children taken by the Amalekites.

Responses to crisis

You can cry

The anguish of David's men was great. The Bible says these mighty men "wept until they had no more power to weep" (1 Sam 30:4).

Have you ever been in, or heard news of, a situation so intensely painful that you wanted to cry? Or perhaps you did cry, even until you were utterly exhausted. Indeed, there are times when there simply are no words to express our pain, grief, anguish, or disappointment. So, we cry. But, when the crying is over, what then?

You can give way to anger, bitterness and hostility

For David's men, grief quickly turned into anger and anger into bitterness and hostility. They no doubt blamed David for provoking the Amalekites in the first place. They blamed him for leaving the women and children defenseless.

The Bible says, "David was greatly distressed, for the men spoke of stoning him because the souls of them all were bitterly grieved, each man for his sons and daughters" (1 Sam 30:6a, AMP). The six hundred mighty men who had fought many successful battles with David as their leader were now ready to throw stones like fastballs at him until he died.

Or, you can encourage yourself in the Lord

Without a doubt, David's situation was intensely stressful. "But David encouraged and strengthened himself in the Lord his God" (1 Sam 30:6b, AMP).

How David encouraged himself

The definition of encourage is to *stimulate the hope of*, to *give confidence or courage to*. The Hebrew root word means to *be firm, strong*, and *courageous to conquer*. David encouraged and strengthened himself in the Lord until he was stimulated with hope and full of courage to conquer.

First, David asked Abiathar the priest to bring the ephod (the high priest's holy garment) so he could inquire of the Lord, literally *seek God's face* for direction. Abiathar brought the ephod to David.

> So David inquired of the Lord, saying, "Shall I pursue this troop? Shall I overtake them?"
>
> And He answered him, "Pursue, for you shall surely overtake them and without fail recover all." ~ 1 Sam 30:8

Second, David believed God would help him recover all. With the Lord of Hosts backing him, David and four hundred of his men pursued the Amalekites, attacked them from twilight until evening of the next day, and recovered everything the Amalekites had stolen. (1 Sam 30:17-19)

The thief

A thief takes what is not legally or rightfully his. Jesus spoke of the devil as "the thief" who comes to steal, and to kill, and to destroy (Jn 10:10).

To steal means *to take the prosperity of others*; to kill is *to deprive of life or the quality of life*; and to destroy is *to put to death or subject to total defeat*.

There are four things the devil will always try to steal from you:

- Your POWER: God's Word, your prayer time, your spirit life, your joy, and your peace;

- Your POSITION: who you are in Christ;

- Your PURPOSE in God; and

- Your POSSESSIONS: spiritual and natural, e.g., family, home, health, and wealth.

These things are yours by the grace of God in, by, and through Christ Jesus. Do not let the devil steal them!

Inquire of the Lord

In the event you have been ripped off by the devil —if he has stolen even one thing God gave to you— take action like David. First, inquire of the Lord regarding the matter.

Unlike the Old Covenant saints, we do not have to go through a priest or any other human agency to inquire of the Lord. Through union with Christ who is our High Priest, every believer has direct access to God anytime day or night.

We can inquire of the Lord through prayer, searching the Scriptures, and listening to the Holy Spirit when he speaks to our heart. (See Heb 4:14-16; Phil 4:6-7; Acts 17:11; Jn 16:13.)

Encourage and strengthen yourself in the Lord

Encourage and strengthen yourself in the Lord until you are *stimulated with hope* and *full of courage to conquer.*

—**Have faith in God**. God is the Creator of the Universe, the giver and sustainer of all life. He upholds all things by the word of His power. Nothing is too difficult for Him. Be fully persuaded that God is able to do *exceedingly abundantly above* all we think or ask. With God all things are possible. (Gen 1:1; Heb 1:3; Eph 3:20; Mk 10:27)

—**Express your confidence in God**. Praise Him for His mighty acts. Praise Him according to His excellent greatness. (Ps 150:2) Declare that your hope and trust is in God alone.

—**Sing songs of deliverance**.

> The Lord is my light and my salvation. Whom shall I fear? The Lord is the strength of my life. Of whom shall I be afraid? ~ Ps 27:1

—**Take action according to the Word of the Lord**. Sometimes God says, "Be still and see the salvation of the Lord." Other times He gives specific instructions for action we need to take toward our own recovery. He might say, "If you do this, then I will do that." Be sensitive to the voice of God for His pathway of recovery for you.

While recovery or replacement of what was stolen from you may not happen immediately, believe that God is working things out for your greatest benefit and His ultimate glory.

> And we know that all things work together for good to those who love God, to those who are the called according to His purpose. ~ Rom 8:28

The Apostle Paul's encouraging words

The Apostle Paul suffered rejection, betrayal, shipwreck, cruel beatings, being stoned and left for dead, and being unjustly thrown in jail. Yet he knew the key to victory was to encourage and strengthen himself in the Lord. Paul wrote:

> We are hard-pressed on every side, yet not crushed; we are perplexed, but not in despair; persecuted, but not forsaken; struck down, but not destroyed ~ 2 Cor 4:8-9

We may be hard-pressed (hedged in) on every side, yet we are not crushed. We are never pressed, squeezed or pounded to the point of destruction.

We may be perplexed (mentally at a loss) but we are never in despair or without hope. We always have hope, because Christ is our hope!

That reminds me of the fact that even a tree that has been cut down has hope.

> For there is hope for a tree, if it is cut down, that it will sprout again, and that its tender

shoots will not cease; though its root may grow old in the earth, and its stump may die in the ground, yet at the scent of water it will bud and bring forth branches like a plant. ~ Job 14:7-8

Your hope is greater than that of a tree. Christ in you, the hope of glory. (Col 1:27)

We may be persecuted (pursued by evil-hearted people and evil forces), but we are not forsaken. For *goodness and mercy shall follow* (run after, chase, and pursue) *us all the days of our life.* (Ps 23:6) And, the Lord Himself has said, "I will never leave you nor forsake you" (Heb. 13:5).

We may get knocked about, battered and bruised, even knocked down, but we are never knocked out.

We may fall down, but we have the power to get back up. Through God's Spirit, His Word, and the love, support and encouragement of God's people, we can not only rise again but rise up stronger than ever before. "A righteous man may fall seven times and rise again...." (Prov 24:16)

We may lose an occasional battle, but we are never defeated, because Christ has already won the war!

Christ is our victory

The Hebrew word for victory is *yasha*. Yasha means *to save, to be open, wide or free, to deliver, help, preserve, save, avenge, defend, rescue,* and *keep safe.* Yasha is the root of Yeshua (Jesus or Joshua). Thus, Yeshua (Jesus) our Savior is our victory!

Yeshua (Jesus) paid the price in full for us to be victorious. He redeemed us by His blood and set us free from sin. He overcame the world for us. He defeated the devil and his evil army. (Col 2:15) He conquered everything that conquered us.

That is why in Christ Jesus we are *more than conquerors*. We are *super victors*, that is, *triumphantly victorious, overwhelmingly victorious* in and through every circumstance.

> Yet in all these things we are more than conquerors through Him who loved us. ~ Rom 8:37

Because we are in Him and He is in us, nothing—no person, devil, angel, other created thing, or circumstance—can separate us from God's love.

> For I am persuaded that neither death nor life, nor angels nor principalities nor powers, nor things present nor things to come, nor height nor depth, nor any other created thing, shall be able to separate us from the love of God that is in Christ Jesus. ~ Rom 8:38-39

God's love for us is lavish, tenacious, immeasurable, and perpetual. Praise the Lord!

Turn stumbling blocks into stepping stones

Smith Wigglesworth said:

> Great faith is the product of great fights. Great testimonies are the outcome of great tests. Great triumphs come only out of great trials. Every stumbling block must become a stepping stone, and every opposition must become an opportunity.

A stumbling block is simply a challenge. We can respond to challenges one of two ways. We can become displeased, indignant or offended by the challenge. Or, we can allow the challenge to become a stepping-stone to go from glory to glory.

Put another way, challenges can trip us up and cause us to fall back, lose ground and remain stagnant. Or they can be the springboards to catapult us to the next level of glory. Just like with King David.

How do we turn stumbling blocks into stepping stones?

> **1. Forgive, forget, and walk in love.**

To forgive means *to let go, lay aside, pardon, release*. Whether a wrong done to us or debt owed to us, simply let it go. Let go of hurt feelings. Let go of the offence. Release the offenders. Then love and bless them. (Mt 5:44)

> **2. Look straight ahead, reach forward to things ahead** (Phil 3:13)

Look straight ahead and reach forward to the things which are ahead. Reach means t*o stretch oneself forward upon something in front.* In other words, forget the small stuff. Concentrate on the vision, destiny, and purpose God has given you.

3. Look straight ahead, press towards the prize (Phil 3:14)

Look straight ahead and press towards the prize. To press means *to pursue* or *follow after*. This carries the idea of having a wholehearted, passionate pursuit. For Christ believers, Christ is the prize.

4. Remember Psalm 119:165

"Great peace have those who love your law, and nothing causes them to stumble." Nothing shall offend them.

Be of good courage

Finally, to those facing a crisis or presently in a difficult situation, King David is shouting out to you: "BE OF GOOD COURAGE, AND HE SHALL STRENGTHEN YOUR HEART, ALL YOU WHO HOPE IN THE LORD" (Ps. 31:24).

Pray, don't faint. Never give up. Encourage yourself in the Lord until you are stimulated with hope and full of courage to conquer!

Key No. 5:

Rely on the Person and Power of the Holy Spirit Within

The key to tapping into supernatural strength, wisdom and power is to rely on the person and power of the Holy Spirit within. This one key will revolutionize your life. It will most certainly give you the strongest tangible sense of victory every day.

The Person of Holy Spirit

The Holy Spirit—

the Spirit of God, the Spirit of Grace, the Spirit of Grace and Supplication, the Spirit of Glory, the Spirit of the Lord, the Spirit of Wisdom, the Spirit of Understanding, the Spirit of Counsel, the Spirit of Might, the Spirit of Knowledge, the Spirit of the Fear of the Lord, the Spirit of Christ, the Eternal Spirit, the Spirit of Truth, the Spirit of Holiness, the Comforter, Spirit of Life in Christ Jesus, the Spirit who raised Christ from the dead, the Promise of the Father, the Holy Ghost, Christ in you the hope of glory.

— delights to work in your life!

[Scripture Ref: Mt 3:16; Heb 10:29; Zech 12:10; 1 Pet 4:14; Is 11:2; Rom 8:9; Heb 9:14; Jn 16:12-14, Jn 14:16, 26; Eph 4:30; Rom 8:2; Rom 8:11; Lk 24:49; Col 1:27]

The Holy Spirit's ministry to you

The Holy Spirit, your Regenerator

As your Regenerator, the Holy Spirit regenerated or recreated your spirit the moment you accepted Christ. You were born again, spiritually born anew from above. The Holy Spirit then took up residence within your spirit. You are now a new creation, a new class of being—a human with a recreated spirit indwelled by the eternal Spirit of God. How awesome is that! (Tit 3:5; 2 Cor 5:17)

> Now we have received, not the spirit of the world, but the Spirit who is from God, that

we might know the things that have been freely given to us by God. ~ 1 Cor 2:12

The Holy Spirit, your divine Helper

And I will pray the Father and He will give you another Helper, that He may abide with you forever ~ Jn 14:16

As your divine Helper (*Parakletos*), the Holy Spirit will give you supernatural help as well as practical day-to-day help the same way Jesus did when he lived among His disciples. He will help you fulfill your purpose.

The Holy Spirit, your Comforter

As your Comforter, the Holy Spirit will comfort, reassure and encourage you in and through distressing situations. He will lead you to the Scriptures you need. He will fill you with supernatural peace.

The Holy Spirit, your Guide

However, when He, the Spirit of Truth, has come, He will guide you into all truth . . . ~ Jn 16:13a

As your Guide, the Holy Spirit, the Spirit of Truth, will show you the way into all truth. He not only bears witness with your spirit that you are a child of God, He will bear witness with your spirit to the authenticity, integrity and truth of God's Word.

> For the Spirit searches all things, yes, the deep things of God. ~ 1 Cor 2:10b

The Holy Spirit guides you primarily through the still small voice of your spirit, the inward witness, divinely inspired impressions, and the fruit of the spirit (*you shall go out with joy and be led forth with peace,* Isa 55:12). He may also speak so clearly inside you that it sounds like an audible voice.

The Holy Spirit, your Counselor

As your Counselor, the Holy Spirit counsels you according to the Holy Scriptures. He is always speaking God's advice to you. You must be still, listen, and heed His counsel.

The Holy Spirit, your Intercessor

As your Intercessor, the Holy Spirit knows the mind and will of God and makes intercession for the saints accordingly. (Rom 8:27)

The Holy Spirit, your Strengthener

As your Strengthener, the Holy Spirit (the Spirit of Might) will strengthen you with miraculous, wonder-working power. The same Holy Spirit who raised Christ from the dead dwells in you and will also revive, stimulate and enliven your mortal body. (Eph 3:16; Rom 8:11)

When you wholeheartedly praise the Lord, The Holy Spirit will give you overflowing joy. "The joy of the Lord is your strength." (Neh 8:10)

Rely on the Person and Power of Holy Spirit Within

The Holy Spirit, your Inside Informer

> . . . For He will not speak on His own authority, but whatever He hears He will speak. ~ Jn 16:13b

As your Inside Informer, the Holy Spirit speaks what He hears in the throne room of God. When He speaks to your heart, He is sending you an instant message, a fresh word from Heaven, from the very heart of God our Father and the Lord Jesus Christ.

The Holy Spirit, your divine Revelator

> . . . And He will tell you things to come. ~ Jn 16:13c

The Bible is a prophetic book, foretelling events hundreds and even thousands of years before they happen. As your divine Revelator, the Holy Spirit will reveal these truths to you. He will also show you events to come in your life.

The Holy Spirit, your divine Teacher

> But the Comforter, which is the Holy Ghost, whom the Father will send in my name, he shall teach you all things, and bring all things to your remembrance, whatsoever I have said unto you. ~ Jn 14:26

As your divine Teacher, the Holy Spirit will explain the Scriptures to you. He will reveal treasures of knowledge and wisdom essential for living. He will teach you how to rightly divide the word of truth—how to distinguish truth from error, grace from legalism.

The Holy Spirit is the Anointing within

The Holy Spirit is the anointing within you.

> But the anointing which you have received from Him abides in you, and you do not need that anyone teach you; but as the same anointing teaches you concerning all things, and is true, and is not a lie, and just as it has taught you, you will abide in Him. ~ 1 Jn 8:27

The anointing is the presence, sparkling life and power of God. The anointing abides in you. You must abide in Him.

The Holy Spirit, Glorifier of Jesus

> He will glorify Me, for He will take of what is Mine and declare it to you. ~ Jn 16:14

The Holy Spirit glorifies the Lord Jesus. To glorify is *to make glorious by bestowing honor, praise, or admiration.* The Holy Spirit will glorify the Lord Jesus and make Him gloriously real to you. He will shine the light on the Lord in all His excellence.

The Holy Spirit, your Personal Transformer

As your Personal Transformer, the Holy Spirit

works in you to will and to do of God's good pleasure. He works in you to produce the fruit and character of Christ. The Holy Spirit works day by day to transform your inner man into the glorious image of Christ. (Phil 2:13; 2 Cor 4:16; 2 Cor 3:18)

The Holy Spirit, your divine Prayer Partner

As your divine Prayer Partner, the Holy Spirit will help you pray, praise and worship. He will help you have intimate fellowship with God. He will help you pray according to the will of God.

Sometimes the Holy Spirit prompts us to pray by giving us thoughts, impressions, a flash of a name or face, a word of knowledge, a word of wisdom, or a dream or vision. Other times, He wakes us up suddenly and impresses us to pray.

The Bible tells us to pray always with all prayer and supplication in the spirit. (Eph 6:18) Praying in the spirit literally means *to pray in the spiritual realm with the Holy Spirit's aid.* When we don't know what to pray, the Holy Spirit will help us. The Holy Spirit knows the mind, heart and will of the Father. He will come to our aid in prayer. He does not pray for us. He helps us to pray effectively.

The Holy Spirit, your supernatural Leader

> For as many as are led by the Spirit of God, they are the sons of God. ~ Rom 8:14

As your supernatural Leader, the Holy Spirit leads you by moving, driving, inducing, guiding, and directing you in your spirit. All who receive Christ are children of God by spiritual rebirth. Those who are led (moved, driven, induced, guided, directed) by the Spirit of God are the mature sons and daughters of God.

It is the mature sons and daughters of God who have learned to follow the leading, prompting, and direction of the Holy Spirit.

Sometimes the Holy Spirit will lead us by moving or impelling us to take some kind of action. Any action prompted by the Holy Spirit will of course always line up with God's Word, His purpose, and His excellent character.

An example of this was when Jesus was led up by the Spirit into the wilderness to be tempted of the devil. Mark's gospel says the Spirit thrust or drove Jesus out into the wilderness. (Mt 4:1; Mk 1:12)

Sometimes the Spirit will lead you to a place of testing as He did when He led Jesus into the wilderness. (More about tests in Chapter 6) Wherever God leads us by His Spirit, we can rest assured that He will help us by the same Spirit.

The Holy Spirit, your Standby

As your Standby, the Holy Spirit stands ready, willing, and able to assist you in whatever situation you are in. He waits for you to ask Him for help.

You are the temple of the Holy Spirit

> Do you not know that your body is the temple (the very sanctuary) of the Holy Spirit Who lives within you, Whom you have received [as a Gift] from God? You are not your own. ~ 1 Cor 6:19 (AMP)

> For you were bought at a price; therefore glorify God in your body and in your spirit, which are God's. ~ 1 Cor 6:20

You are the temple, the sanctuary, the dwelling place for the Spirit of God in the earth. He is with you wherever you go. Selah.

> Now the Lord is the Spirit; and where the Spirit of the Lord is, there is liberty. ~ 2 Cor 3:17

Be ever filled with the Spirit

> And do not be drunk with wine, in which is dissipation, but be filled with the Spirit. ~ Eph 5:18

To be filled with the Spirit means to live each day under the controlling influence of the Holy Spirit and the inexhaustible mighty power inherent in Christ.

The Amplified Bible says to "ever be filled and stimulated" with the Spirit. Wuest says, "constantly, consciously, definitely subject to the Spirit, a life that has a consuming desire for His control over every thought, word, and deed, thus a life unceasingly controlled by the Spirit."

Be enthusiastic. Enthused in the Greek is en Theos, which means *full of God*. When we are full of God, enthusiasm will be the outflow.

Without a doubt, the quality of your outward life depends on the quality of your inner life. Guard your heart. Build up your inner man through God's Word, prayer, praise, and worship.

Be aware of and sensitive to the revelation, witness, voice, wooing, leading and constraints of the Holy Spirit within. Yield to Him. Be filled, possessed, and led by Him.

Power of the Holy Spirit

The eternal omnipresent, omnipotent, omniscient Spirit of God, co-creator of the universe, lives in you! He is far greater than any created thing. "You are of God, little children, and have overcome them because greater is He that is in you than He that is in the world" (1 Jn 4:4). The Spirit of Might lives inside you!

Yes indeed. You have a reservoir of treasures, riches, sparkling life and power inside you in the person of the Holy Spirit.

Always remember that God "is able to do exceedingly abundantly above all that we ask or think according to the power that works in us" (Eph 3:20).

Key No. 6:

Consider it Pure Joy

> Consider it pure joy, my brothers and sisters, whenever you face trials of many kinds, because you know that the testing of your faith produces perseverance. Let perseverance finish its work so that you may be mature and complete, not lacking anything. ~ Jas 1:2-4 (NIV)

If you consider it pure joy when you face various trials, and cheerfully persevere through them, God promises you will come out victorious—mature, complete, not lacking or deficient in anything!

Two kinds of tests

Naturally and spiritually, a test is a set of circumstances or problems that prove, examine, and scrutinize a person's knowledge, abilities, or character.

Generally speaking, when something is tested, it is to determine or prove its legitimacy. Is it really what it is supposed to be? Is its composition and strength as is claimed?

There are two kinds of tests that Christ Believers experience. One is temptations or solicitations to do evil. Solicitations to do evil do not come from God.

> Let no man say when he is tempted, 'I am tempted by God'; for God cannot be tempted by evil, nor does He himself tempt anyone. ~ Jas 1:13

The tempter is Satan. He came in the form of a serpent to Eve in the Garden of Eden. He tempted Jesus in the wilderness. He works with a host of wicked spirits to tempt Christ believers to do wrong. (1 Thess 3:5; Gen 3:1; Mt 4; Eph 6:12)

The other kind of test is comprised of various trials such as persecution, afflictions and troubles. This chapter is about tests of this kind.

However, no matter the temptation, test or trial you face, if you will stay full of the Holy Spirit, hold fast to God's Word, keep your joy, and do the right thing (what wisdom and prudence demands in your situation), you will come out victorious.

The ultimate purpose of trials

> that the genuineness of your faith, being much more precious than gold that perishes, though it is tested by fire, may be found to praise, honor, and glory at the revelation of Jesus Christ. ~ 1 Pet 1:7

The ultimate purpose of the trials we face in life is to prove the genuineness of our faith. Trials reveal the depth of one's character, resolve, love and commitment to Christ, and faithfulness to God's Word.

The process of testing and showing that your faith is genuine is abundantly more precious than testing gold, the most precious of metals. Gold is tested by fire to determine its purity and value. John Clarke wrote:

> Through fire, gold is separated from all alloy and heterogeneous mixtures and is proved to be gold by its enduring the action of the fire without losing anything of its nature, weight, color, or any other property.

Gold emerges out of the refiner's fire purged of impurities. The purer it is the more valuable it is. Yet, no matter how precious pure gold is, it is not indestructible or imperishable.

On the other hand, every time Christ believers go through the refiner's fire with cheerful endurance, we are cleansed from impurities of heart. Our faith is tested and proved genuine.

Greater still, nothing is lost in our nature or other property. In fact, after the test we are better—stronger in character, virtue, strength, and resolve. More precious than gold!

Spiritual sequence when you hear God's Word

Every time you hear God's Word a spiritual sequence takes place. Locate yourself in the sequence and you will know precisely what to do to press through to victory.

1. The Word comes.

Every Scripture is *God-breathed*, full of life, energy, and miraculous power. God's Word is truth. The Word is designed to accomplish what God sent it to do. (2 Tim 3:16; Jn 17:17; Is 55:11) When you hear God's Word and receive it into your heart . . .

2. Faith comes.

> So then faith comes by hearing and hearing by the Word of God.~ Rom 10:17

Faith is a powerful living force that comes from our heart or spirit.

God put a share of faith in our spirit when we were born again. ". . . God has dealt to each one the measure of faith." (Rom 12:3)

We are saved by grace through faith. By faith we access God's grace and all the blessings, resources and divine privileges that belong to us in, by and through Christ Jesus. (Eph 2:8; Rom 5:2)

To believe and to have faith are essentially two sides to the same coin. Believe means *to trust in, have faith in, be fully convinced of, acknowledge,* and *rely on*. Faith means *firm persuasion, conviction,* and *assurance*.

In Colossians faith is described as "that leaning of the entire human personality on Him in absolute trust and confidence in His power, wisdom, and goodness." (Col 2:4, AMP)

Hebrews 11:1 tells us that faith is present tense (*now*). The time to believe God's Word with all our heart is the moment we hear it.

By combining the principles of Romans 10:10, 2 Corinthians 4:13, and James 2:17, we discover a formula to operate in living faith:

> Heart belief + spoken confession + corresponding action (based on God's Word) = Living Faith

After faith comes, then . . .

3. Satan comes.

Satan comes to steal the Word from you. He brings pressures such as persecutions, troubles, and solicitations to do evil to get you to back off the Word.

Persecution means *to be pursued, to be hounded,*

put to flight, driven away, chased, and *harassed*. Satan and his demonic forces are always pursuing, harassing, nipping at the heels of God's people, always trying to pressurize us to focus on things other than God's Word.

Persecutions and pressures arise to cast a shadow of doubt on God's Word. If Satan can steal the Word from you, then you have nothing on which to base your faith.

The devil is not able to steal the Word from all believers. Jesus explains how the devil is able to steal the Word from some.

Seed scattered by the roadside

> When anyone hears the word of the Kingdom, and doesn't understand it, the evil one comes, and snatches away that which has been sown in his heart. This is what was sown by the roadside. ~ Mt 13:19 (WEB).

When a person casually or nonchalantly hears God's Word without seeking to understand it with his or her heart, the devil can snatch away the Word that was sown.

Have you ever gone home after church service and immediately plopped down to watch a movie, sports event, or some other thing on television? As you give attention to the television program, the message you heard at church soon becomes a faint memory. Someone could ask you an hour later what was preached, and you cannot remember. Oh, you know the Word was good—but for some reason you cannot remember one point.

The fact is the Word never traveled from your outer ear to your inner ear and down into your spirit where it could take root and grow. Thus, the Word you heard did not produce any fruit in your life.

On the other hand, when you pay attention to the Word you hear, seek to understand it, hold fast to your confession of faith (Heb 10:23; 35-36), and continue believing that what God promised to you belongs to you, then . . .

4. Perseverance comes.

Your faith will activate the powerful force of perseverance. (Jas 1:3) As you stand firm on and declare God's Word, perseverance comes to undergird your faith and help you stand firm footed and resolute.

Perseverance is a discipline of the soul. It is comprised of *determination, persistency, steadfast courage,* and *cheerful constant endurance.* It is a hang-tough attitude that will not surrender to circumstances nor succumb to trial.

Perseverance says: "Since you believe God's promise, hold fast and continue believing Him, and you will experience the promise."

This is the pivotal point that determines whether or not you experience what you believe God for. Do not give in to doubt, fear, or unbelief. You must hold fast to and declare God's Word no matter what.

The Lord Jesus says:

> . . . Assuredly, I say to you, if you have faith as a mustard seed, you will say to this mountain, 'Move from here to there,' and it will move; and nothing will be impossible for you.

If you have faith the size of a tiny mustard seed you have enough faith to move mountains. Metaphorically, mountains are seemingly insurmountable obstacles. The Lord is saying that if you have even the tiniest bit of faith you have the power to move seemingly insurmountable obstacles in your life. "And nothing will be impossible to you" (Mt 17:20).

Stand in faith, hold fast to and declare God's Word, control your soul, release some joy, and wait on the Lord.

To wait on the Lord means to look with eager and confident expectation for the fulfillment of God's promise. It also means to be *entwined together* (with the Lord) like the threads in a tightly twisted rope.

In other words, stay in tight, intimate fellowship with the Lord. Purpose that you will not be moved, pressed or driven to do anything outside the will and timing of God. Stay determined to be led only by the Holy Spirit and God's Word.

So then, faith activates perseverance. Perseverance undergirds and strengthens faith. The end result of perseverance is that . . .

5. Experience comes.

If you count it all joy when going through trials

and tests of faith, if you hold steadfast to God's Word and let perseverance have its perfect work or result, you will experience what you believe God for. And, you will be perfect, complete, lacking nothing! Then, after experience . . .

6. Hope comes.

Once you experience the fulfillment of God's promise, then it will be easy to have hope the next time you face a similar situation. God has proven His faithfulness to you. Now your hope is strong that He will come through for you again and again.

The apostle Paul wrote:

> ...we also glory in tribulations, knowing that tribulation produces perseverance; and perseverance, character; and character, hope. ~ Rom 5:3-4

We can glory in times of trouble and pressure because we know that trouble and pressure activate and develop perseverance. Perseverance produces character. Character produces hope. And, hope is an anchor of our souls. (Heb 6:19)

Jesus, our example of joyful perseverance

Christ of eternity, called the Word of God, became flesh and dwelt among us as Jesus of Nazareth. (Jn 1:14) Jesus is our example of joyful perseverance.

If you were God, would you leave your throne of glory in Heaven to come to earth to die for the sins of humanity? Would you divest yourself of your divine privileges, rights and power to condescend to take on mortal flesh, live as a servant, suffer rejection of kinfolk, hostility of sinners, allow yourself to be brutally beaten, scourged, violently nailed to a cross, have the sins of billions of people laid on you, and die for all those people? That is just a thumbnail of what Jesus did for humanity.

Jesus was able to endure and go through it all because he kept His focus and joy.

> Looking unto Jesus, the author and finisher of our faith, who for the joy that was set before Him endured the cross, despising the shame, and has sat down at the right hand of the throne of God ~ Heb 12:2-3

The sinless Lamb of God chose to suffer and die to pay the penalty for our sins. He knew that his suffering and death on the cross would result in billions of people being eternally saved.

Jesus looked past the shame of the cross to the glorious throne room of God. He saw Himself restored to His pre-incarnate majesty, glory, honor, and power. He also saw countless numbers of believers rejoicing with the heavenly host and worshipping God.

Zephaniah prophesied:

> The Lord your God in your midst, The Mighty One, will save; He will rejoice over

you with gladness, He will quiet you with His love, He will rejoice over you with singing." ~ Zeph 3:17

Our light affliction

Certainly, our greatest suffering cannot be compared to what our Lord endured for us. Nor can it be compared to the trials, afflictions, and persecution suffered by Christians throughout the ages and in many parts of the world today.

The apostle Paul, who himself suffered many trials and afflictions, called our afflictions *light*. "For our light affliction, which is but for a moment, is working for us a far more exceeding and eternal weight of glory" (2 Cor 4:17).

You may be facing some significant challenges. In the natural, you do not know how you will make it through. How can anyone think your suffering is light? It certainly does not feel light.

However, no matter what we go through, it is lightweight in view of eternal glory. Eternity is time without end. If one lives one hundred years or more on the earth, what is that compared to eternity?

Our life on earth is temporary. Our troubles are temporary. No, troubles don't last always. That means they have an expiration date. Certainly, our joyous seasons far outnumber periodic seasons of trials.

Ultimately we must be like our Savior and look

past any temporary trouble to the joy set before us—glorification and spending eternity with God and a glorious company of saints from all the ages.

Victory in Christ

In the meantime, we possess everything we need to persevere through every adversity of life. While being a Christ believer does not exempt us from adversities and trials of life, we have spiritual advantages that people in the world do not have. We have Christ.

Therefore, always remember that Daddy God:

—loves you with an everlasting love

—is good (all the time)

—is gracious, full of compassion

—is excellent in all His ways

—is faithful to keep His promises

—will never allow you to be tempted, tested or tried more than you can handle

—will always provide a way to escape (1 Cor 10:13).

Whatever the circumstances (the temporary tough times), consider it pure joy. In actuality, you do not have trouble—you have grand opportunities to show off and declare the love, goodness, faithfulness, and favor of God.

Key No. 7:

Rejoice

> Rejoice in the Lord always. Again, I will say, rejoice. ~ Phil 4:4

The key to releasing the glory and favor of God in your life is to always rejoice in the Lord.

When Mary received God's Word that she would conceive the Christ child by the power of the Holy Spirit, she rejoiced and said, "My soul magnifies the Lord, and my spirit has rejoiced in God my Savior."

One's soul is always supposed to magnify (*enlarge, make great*) the Lord, not the circumstances. The NEB Bible translates Luke 1:46 as: "Tell out my soul the greatness of God." One's spirit, in vital union with God, should always rejoice (joy over and over again), literally *jump for joy*, in God our Savior.

Joy is already in your spirit

Joy is part of the fruit of our recreated spirit. Joy is love exalted, leaping out in delight and gladness, in success and victory.

We were created to proclaim and show forth the excellent virtues of the Lord. We were made to acclaim, applaud, boast about, congratulate, extol, magnify, celebrate, and salute the Lord who is exceedingly great and exceedingly greatly to be praised.

God is our Savior. The spiritual kingdom of God (*righteousness, peace and joy in the Holy Spirit*) is inside us. The spirit of triumph is inside us.

Joy in the midst of adversity

> Although the fig tree may not blossom, nor fruit be on the vines; though the labor of the olive may fail and the fields yield no food, though the flock may be cut off from the field and there be no heard in the stalls, yet I will rejoice in the Lord, I will joy in the God of my salvation. ~ Hab 3:17-19

We may not find joy in the circumstances, but we can always find joy in the Lord.

Christians in the early church knew how to keep their joy in the midst of adversity. They knew how to rejoice in the Lord, our Savior.

Peter and John were beaten for preaching in the Name of Jesus. Instead of complaining and feeling sorry for themselves, they rejoiced that they were "counted worthy to suffer shame for His name" (Acts 5:40-41).

Paul and Silas were beaten and thrown in jail after casting out a spirit of divination from a young woman. They did not let that steal their joy. "But at midnight Paul and Silas were praying and singing hymns to God, and the prisoners were listening to them."

Their praise was powerfully triumphant because "Suddenly, there was a great earthquake, and the prison was shaken to its foundations. All the doors flew open, and the chains of every prisoner fell off!" (Acts 16:22-26)

The key to being able to rejoice in the midnight hour is to habitually start each day with praise.

From the rising of the sun, rejoice

In the Old Testament God had a prescribed arrangement for the twelve tribes of Israel to pitch their tents and encamp around the tabernacle. The tribe of Judah (Judah means *celebrate* or *praise*) was set up "on the east side toward the rising of the sun" (Num 2:3).

The sun rising in the East signifies the beginning of a new day. Each day should begin with celebration, praise, thanksgiving, and rejoicing in the Lord.

> This is the day the Lord has made. We will rejoice and be glad in it. ~ Ps 118:24
>
> I will bless the Lord at all times; His praise shall continually be in my mouth. ~ Ps 34:1
>
> I will praise Him for His mighty acts. I will praise Him according to His excellent greatness. ~ 150:2

Start the day with thanksgiving and praise

> [It is] good to give thanks to the LORD, and to sing praises to Your name, O Most High; to declare Your loving-kindness in the morning, and Your faithfulness every night. ~ Ps 92:1-12

It is good to give thanks to the Lord. The Amplified version says *good and delightful*. It is good and delightful to start the day with thanksgiving.

In Psalm 100, worshippers are exhorted: "Enter into His gates with thanksgiving and into His courts with praise . . ." (Ps 100:4).

We should thank the Lord because He is good. He paid the price for you and me to have a plethora of fantastic benefits.

I am reminded of how much I like to give and receive gift cards. Most times when people give me gift cards I hold onto them until a day when I especially feel like treating myself. What is so nice about a gift card is that I did not have to pay anything for it. Someone else purchased it and then gave it to me. All I do is say "thank you," use the card, and enjoy its benefits.

And, so, each, day we awake to a fully loaded divine benefit card. All we have to do is say, "Thank You, Lord."

> Thank You, Lord, for your loving kindness and tender mercies over my life today.
>
> Thank You for food, health, strength and vitality.
>
> Thank You, Lord, for a roof over my head and a floor under my feet.
>
> Thank You for my family.
>
> Thank You for salvation.
>
> Thank You for delivering me from the power of darkness.
>
> Thank You for daily restoring my soul.
>
> Thank You for the peace of God that rules my life.
>
> Thank You for Your amazing grace.
>
> Thank You for Your indescribable gift in

my Lord and Savior, Jesus Christ.

[Scripture refs: Ps 92:2; Ps 106:1; Ps 145:9; Ps 68:19; Ps 103:4; Col 2:13-15; Ps 23:3; Col 3:15; 1 Cor 1:4; 2 Cor 9:15]

Thank God when you pray

> Be anxious for nothing, but in everything by prayer and supplication, with thanksgiving, let your requests be made known to God ~ Phil 4:6

In everything give thanks

> In everything give thanks, for this is the will of God in Christ Jesus concerning you. ~ 1 Thess 5:18

Giving thanks in everything is the highest expression of faith and is the will of God for you and me. No matter what the circumstance, no matter what you are going through, you can lift up your hands, open your mouth, and give God thanks.

> Even if my body is racked with pain, I will thank and praise the Lord my Healer. (Yahweh Rapha)

> Even if my bank account is down to pennies, I will thank and praise the Lord my Provider (*Yahweh Yireh*). I will thank and praise the Lord who is my peace and prosperity (*Yahweh Shalom*).

Rejoice

Even when I have been done horribly wrong, I will thank and praise the Lord that goodness and mercy shall follow me all the days of my life. (Ps 23:6)

We are to continually offer to God a sacrifice of praise, "which is the fruit of our lips giving thanks to His name." (Heb 13:15)

The results of rejoicing in the Lord

God is enthroned in, inhabits, and dwells in our praises. As we praise Him, He fills the temple, which temple we are. We are infused with more of His life, love, joy, peace, and amazing grace.

Praise will:

1. Prepare you to hear God's voice in your inner man.

2. Prepare you to digest God's Word.

3. Change the spiritual climate around you. Putting on praise like a garment will displace the spirit of heaviness.

4. Silence the avenger.

5. Put things in proper perspective—big God, little problem.

6. Encourage one's heart.

7. Edify one's spirit.

8. Calm one's soul.

The best way to keep joy is to develop a habit of praising the Lord every day.

[Scripture refs: Ps 8:2; Is 61:3; 2 Chron 20:21; Acts 16:25-26; Ps 22:3]

Thank God for victory

> Thanks be to God, who gives us the victory through our Lord Jesus Christ. ~ 1 Cor 15:57

> Now thanks be to God who always leads us in triumph in Christ, and through us diffuses the fragrance of His knowledge in every place. ~ 2 Cor 2:14

***

Heartfelt rejoicing, praise and thanksgiving are sure-fire ways to bless God, shut down the operations of the enemy in our lives, and energize one's day for Spirit-infused joyous and victorious living.

Key No. 8:

Realize You Are Unique, Gifted and Qualified

Realizing that you are unique, gifted and qualified is an important key to living in victory every day and discovering and fulfilling your life's purpose.

When you know who you are and who God has called and qualified you to be, you will possess an unshakable confidence, strength and energy. You will wake up every day with a strong sense of purpose.

You are Unique

Unique means *one of a kind, rare, uncommon*. You are one of a kind. God made you different from others in a way that makes you special and worthy of note.

The current world population is 7 billion, 220 million people, and counting. (*See* http://www.worldometers.info/world-population). Yet, while billions of people live and have lived on the earth, there is and never has been anybody exactly like you.

Nobody else has your exact DNA (genetic blueprint, code or map). No one else has fingerprints like you. By God's creation and design, you are unique, rare and uncommon!

Fearfully and wonderfully made

Musing on the awesomeness of God's omniscience and amazing intricate work in creating him made David break out into praise: "I will praise You, for I am fearfully and wonderfully made." (Ps 139:14)

Today, through ultrasound imaging we can view a fetus in the womb at different stages of development.

> At 4 weeks "the baby is developing the structures that will eventually form his face and neck. The heart and blood vessels continue to develop. And the lungs, stomach, and liver start to develop."
>
> . . .
>
> At 16 weeks, "the baby now measures about 4.3 to 4.6 inches and weighs about 3.5 ounces... The baby's eyes can blink and the

heart and blood vessels are fully formed. The baby's fingers and toes have fingerprints."

At 20 weeks, the baby "can suck a thumb, yawn, stretch, and make faces . . ."

(http://www.webmd.com/baby/ss/slideshow-fetal-development)

Think about it. God knew before your mother's egg was penetrated and fertilized by your father's sperm what you would look like in every stage of development pre and post birth. And He knew what you would grow up to become.

God told Jeremiah that before he was in his mother's womb God knew him and ordained him a prophet. (Jer 1:5)

That tells me that God has a plan and purpose for every one of us that precedes our parents meeting and coming together. That tells me that the circumstances surrounding a person's conception and birth are really irrelevant.

You were not an accident. You were born at precisely the right time according to God's timetable.

The outward circumstances regarding your birth do not matter. Maybe you were adopted and do not know your natural parents. The Bible says, "When my father and my mother forsake me, then the Lord will take care of me" (Ps 27:10). One of the ways He takes care of you is to give you loving parents to take care of you and help you become what God intended.

Even if you were abandoned, forsaken, neglected or mistreated by people who were supposed to take care of you, know that God's love, original intent and purpose for you has never changed.

God is way more interested in your success than you are. His thoughts towards you are precious (weighty), way more than can be numbered or measured.

> How precious also are your thoughts to me, O God! How great is the sum of them! ~ Ps 139:17

Beloved, God planned for you to live in this generation before you were ever conceived. You were destined for such a time as this. And, you are fearfully and wonderfully made. You are unique.

God fashioned your inner self like no other

> The Lord looks down from heaven and sees every person. From his throne he watches all who live on earth. He made [fashions all] their hearts and understands everything they do. ~ Ps 33:13-15 (EXB)

God fashioned your inner self like no other. Your soul (mind, will, emotions, personality) is uniquely you. Nobody just like you! That tells me that you have a way of seeing things, a way of doing things, a way of expressing things like no one else.

You are an original. Yes, you are indeed a *piece of work*. You are God's masterpiece.

> For we are His workmanship, created in Christ Jesus for good works, which God prepared beforehand that we should walk in them ~ Eph 2:10

Unique gifts and talents

God endowed you with unique gifts and talents.

Grace gifts

Every person is endowed with at least one gift of grace or grace-ability. The Greek call it *charisma*.

A charisma is a *spiritual endowment*, a *miraculous faculty*, *a free gift*, a gift of God's grace. It is an innate gift, inherent in one's nature.

It is sometimes called a *joy gift* (the root of charisma is charis which means *joy*). This is a gift that brings you the greatest joy when you operate in it.

A charisma is sometimes called a *motivation gift* because the gift is a strong motivating force within.

A charisma is also called a *foundation gift* because it forms a strong foundation or fundamental part of one's personality.

Seven gifts of grace (charismata) are listed in Romans 12:6-8. (Throughout Scripture the number seven signifies divine perfection, revelation, fullness, and completion.) The seven charismata with a brief description are as follows:

Prophecy: Here, one is graced or endowed with a gift of ongoing prophetic insight and forthright speaking ability.

This gift is different from the supernatural bubbling forth of prophecy as one of the nine manifestations of the Holy Spirit described in 1 Corinthians 12:7. Nor does having this gift mean that one is called to the office of a prophet (Eph 4:11).

Serving: The one so gifted likes to aid, serve, offer relief to meet the practical needs of others. A server is a hands-on, task oriented kind of person. In the church they are called deacons.

Teaching: The ones so gifted love to help others understand. They love to explain. They usually love to study and research. Ask them (people like me) what kind of books they like to read and the list usually is top heavy with encyclopedias, word studies, and dictionaries.

One may have a general teaching gift, or one might be called to the five-fold ministry as a teacher to the Body of Christ.

Exhortation: The one with this gift loves to encourage, inspire and motivate others. A hallmark expression is: "I just want to encourage you . . ." Positive, people oriented, practical.

Giving: The one with this gift loves to share, impart, and give (time, talent, and treasures) to benefit others.

Leading: The one with this gift has the ability to

and loves to inspire, motivate, organize, and direct others.

Shows mercy: The one with this gift responds with great compassion to the distress of others.

Again, every person has at least one of these God-given gifts. You may have a combination of gifts. The gift(s) will operate and be expressed differently through each person's unique personality.

We are born with these gifts. When we receive Christ as Savior and are born again, the Holy Spirit clarifies our gifts and calling, anoints us and helps us use our God-given gifts to fulfill our destiny.

Have you discovered your motivation gift(s)? Continue reading for seven questions you can ask yourself to help you identify your gift(s).

Seven questions to ask yourself to discover your God-given gifts

Here are seven questions to ask yourself to help you identify your God-given gifts. Listen to your spirit. Write the questions, pray, and then write your divinely inspired impressions.

1. What is it I love to do?
2. What is it I do that evokes in me the most enthusiasm and joy?
3. What activity gives me the greatest sense of God's peace?
4. What flows naturally (easy as breathing)?
5. What is it I do that always produces good fruit?

6. What is it that others (especially mature Christians) see in me?

7. What is it that I could enthusiastically devote the rest of my life to doing?

God will give you answers. He will speak to your heart. He will lead you in His Word.

He may also speak to you through dreams and visions. He may send people to confirm what you already sense or know about your gifts.

Journal everything you sense is relevant. Visit your journal often.

The purpose of God-given gifts

The purpose of God-given gifts is to win the lost, to build up the church, to glorify God, and to meet one's temporal needs.

While many books have been written about personality types based on science or temporal knowledge, the seven gifts in Romans 12:6-8 are based on revelation knowledge. God reveals His gifts to us.

These gifts of grace are foundationally and fundamentally part of our personality and motivation and will bring us the greatest joy when we operate in them. They were designed by God to be part of our unique spiritual I.D. and to be used to fulfill our destiny.

Stir up the gift of God in you

> "Therefore, I remind you to stir up the gift of God which is in you." ~ 2 Tim 1:6

Once you identify your God-given gifts, begin to develop and use them. The Bible says to stir up the gift of God in you. To stir up is to *fan into flames*, to *rekindle the fire*, to *keep passion alive*. Be passionate about your God-given gifts and talents.

Use your gifts according to God's purpose for your life-work and ministry. The Apostle Peter says: "As each one has received a gift [charisma], minister it to one another, as good stewards of the manifold grace of God." (1 Pet 4:10).

You are qualified

From God's standpoint, you are qualified to do whatever He has gifted and called you to do. Romans 11:29 tells us the gifts and calling of God are *irrevocable*. God never changes his mind or takes back his gifts and calling.

From our standpoint, we have to grow up spiritually. We have to develop our character as well as our gifts. It is by reason of use, over time, that we are able to establish our unique I.D. in Christ.

Declare your uniqueness

You are God's unique creation, fearfully and wonderfully made. His thoughts towards you are precious (weighty). They cannot be counted or measured.

Acknowledge the good things in you and declare your uniqueness:

"I am fearfully and wonderfully made. I am unique in God's eyes. I am a new creation. I carry the wonderful presence of God within me. I am the temple of the Holy Spirit. I carry God's gifts, His grace, His power, His fruit, His character, His wisdom. I carry His eternal purpose within me." (Ps 139:14, 1 Cor 6:19; 1 Cor 1:30)

Pursue God's purpose for your life

When we know our unique I.D., gifts and calling, we can begin to discover and pursue God's purpose for our lives.

If you are an older person and do not know what God's purpose is for your life, you can start now to discover it. So long as you are alive, you carry the purpose and dreams that God put within you to fulfill.

Some of you know your purpose. You just need to get re-focused and make the adjustments necessary to get on the right track.

Pray and begin to do what God speaks to your heart. Then, like King David, serve your generation by the will of God. (Acts 13:36)

You will have the greatest joy and sense of victory when you lay hold to your unique I.D. and move forward in God's perfect path of peace and liberty for you. You will start to do what you love and love what you do. A victorious state of mind every day!

Key No. 9:

Reign Through Heaven's Eyes

The key to reigning in life is to view all of life through Heaven's eyes. From Heaven's point of view, you have power over every opposition. In Christ you are a *super victor*. You can reign in life because:

1. **You are a child of God.**

    For you are all sons of God through faith in Christ Jesus. ~ Gal 3:26

2. **This is your Father's universe.**

    The earth is the Lord's, and all its fullness,

the world and those who dwell therein. ~ Ps 24:1

3. **The universe is upheld by Christ who is seated at the right hand of God the Father.**

   who being the brightness of His glory and the express image of His person, and upholding all things by the word of His power, when He had by Himself purged our sins, sat down at the right hand of the Majesty on high ~ Heb 1:3

4. **The Lord God omnipotent reigns.**

   The Lord has established His throne in heaven, and His kingdom rules over all. ~ Ps 103:19

   Your throne, O God, is forever and ever; a scepter of righteousness is the scepter of your kingdom. ~ Heb 1:8

   Alleluia! For the Lord God Omnipotent reigns! ~ Rev 19:6b

   God's throne is established in Heaven. He reigns forever and ever.

5. **Christ is exalted Lord over all.**

   Yours, O Lord, is the greatness, the power and the glory, the victory and the majesty; for all that is in heaven and in earth is

> yours; yours is the kingdom, O Lord, and you are exalted as head over all. ~1 Chron 29:11

> And every creature which is in heaven and on the earth and under the earth and such as are in the sea, and all that are in them, I heard saying: "Blessing and honor and glory and power be to Him who sits on the throne, and to the Lamb, forever and ever!" ~ Rev 5:13

6. Christ defeated the devil and disarmed principalities and powers.

> Having disarmed principalities and powers, He made a public spectacle of them, triumphing over them in it. ~ Col 2:15

Christ defeated the devil at the cross. He disarmed principalities and powers, so they have no legal right in your life.

7. Christ overcame the world for us.

> I have told you these things, so that in me you may have [perfect] peace and confidence. In this world you have tribulation and trials and distress and frustration; but be of good cheer [take courage; be confident, certain, undaunted]! For I have overcome the world. [I have deprived it of power to harm you and have conquered it for

you.] ~ Jn 16:33 (AMP)

To overcome means to *conquer, subdue, prevail, get the victory, carry off the victory,* and *come off victorious.* The Greek word for "overcome" is the same for "victory." Christ overcame the world for us. He is our victory.

8. **Jesus Christ has all authority in heaven and earth.**

   And Jesus came and spoke to them, saying, "All authority has been given to me in heaven and on earth." ~ Mt 28:18

9. **The Name of Jesus is the most powerful name in the universe.**

   Therefore God has also highly exalted Him and given Him the name which is above every name, that at the name of Jesus every knee should bow, of those in heaven, and of those on earth, and of those under the earth, and that every tongue should confess that Jesus Christ is Lord, to the glory of God the Father. ~ Phil 2:9-11

10. **Your citizenship is in heaven.**

    For our citizenship is in heaven, from which we also eagerly wait for the Savior, the Lord Jesus Christ ~ Phil 3:20

> Now, therefore, you are no longer strangers and foreigners, but fellow citizens with the saints and members of the household of God ~ Eph. 2:19

Generally speaking, a person's allegiance is to the country of their origin or where they obtained citizenship. Being a citizen gives a person rights, privileges not afforded to non-citizens.

Christ believers have dual citizenship. As citizens of earth, we have privileges in the country we were born or to which we repatriated. Of course, in these last days, people's individual freedoms are slipping away more and more as self-centered corrupt and godless political leaders govern the nations.

As citizens of Heaven, Christ believers have true unalienable rights. We have a guarantee of eternal life and all of the blessings of the God quality of life.

11. You have a position of authority with Christ in the heavenly places.

> And raised us up together, and made us sit together in the heavenly places in Christ Jesus. ~ Eph 2:6

> far above all principalities and power and might and dominion; and every name that is named, not only in this age but also in that which is to come; ~ Eph 1:21

God raised us up together with Christ and made us sit together with Him in heavenly places, far above all authorities, principalities, powers, might, and dominion that operate in the lower heavens and atmosphere around us.

12. You have authority to use the Name of Jesus.

You have power of attorney to use the Name of Jesus to bring the righteous policies of Heaven to bear in the earth. You have authority to enforce Christ's victory over the devil.

You have authority to prophesy to principalities and powers the manifold wisdom of God, to tell out the greatness of God. (Eph 3:10)

You have authority to *bind and loose*, that is, to declare spiritual activity as either lawful or unlawful according to God's Word. (Mt 16:19)

You have authority to speak to mountains (obstacles and seemingly insurmountable circumstances), to prophesy the Word of the Lord, and to declare: "As in Heaven, so in earth." (*See* Mt 6:10.)

13. The Spirit of Life in Christ Jesus has made you free from the law of sin and death.

> For the law of the Spirit of life in Christ Jesus has made me free from the law of sin and death. ~ Rom 8:2

You are free from guilt, condemnation, shame, disgrace, fear, bondage, weakness, inability, and the devil's rule over your life.

14. You are more than a conqueror through Christ.

> Yea in all these things we are more than conquerors through Him who loved us. ~ Rom 8:37

Because Christ has conquered everything that was contrary to us, we are more than conquerors (super victors) in, by and through Him.

15. You can overcome anything through faith in God and the power of the Holy Spirit.

> For whatever is born of God overcomes the world. And this is the victory that has overcome the world—our faith. ~ 1 Jn 5:4

> You are of God, little children, and have overcome them, because He who is in you is greater than he who is in the world. ~ 1 Jn 4:4

16. You are kept by the power of God.

> Who are kept by the power of God through faith for salvation ready to be revealed in the last time. ~ 1 Pet 1:5

17. You have holy angels to minister on your behalf.

The Bible reveals that God's holy angels are ministering spirits sent forth from God to minister for the heirs of salvation. They serve as watcher (guardian) angels, messengers, and warriors against the forces of darkness.

> Are they not all ministering spirits sent forth to minister for those who will inherit salvation? ~ Heb 1:14

> For He shall give His angels charge over you, to keep you in all your ways. ~ Ps 91:11

> Bless the Lord, you His angels, who excel in strength, who do His word, heeding the voice of His word. ~ Ps 103:20

18. You have eternal life.

> These things I have written to you who believe in the name of the Son of God, that you may know that you have eternal life, and that you may continue to believe in the name of the Son of God. ~ 1 Jn 5:13

19. You are destined to be conformed to the image of Christ.

> Moreover whom He foreknew, He also predestined to be conformed to the image of His Son, that He might be the firstborn among many brethren. Moreover whom He predestined, these He also called, whom He called, these He also justified; and whom He justified, these He also glorified. ~ Rom 8:29-30

20. Every Christ Believer is being changed into the image of God.

Though our outward man is perishing, our inner man is being renewed day by day. We are being changed by the Spirit of God into the image of God—like when man was first created. We are being changed into the likeness of Christ. (2 Cor. 4:16; Gen. 1:26)

21. You possess the eternal kingdom of God.

You possess the eternal kingdom of God. The kingdom of God is irreplaceable, unshakable, and everlasting.

You have a foretaste of the kingdom within you—righteousness, peace, and joy in the Holy Spirit. (Rom 14:17)

You are also a king under the King of kings and Lord of lords. You can rule, command, and dominate circumstances through God's Word.

22. You have all things present and to come.

In Christ, all things are yours, "whether . . . the world or life or death, or things present or things to come—all are yours. And you are Christ's, and Christ is God's." (1 Cor 3:22-23)

> He who did not spare His own Son, but delivered Him up for us all, how shall He not with Him also freely give us all things? ~ Rom 8:32

23. God has already blessed you with all things that pertain to life and godliness.

> as His divine power has given to us all things that pertain to life and godliness, through the knowledge of Him who called us by glory and virtue, by which have been given to us exceedingly great and precious promises, that through these you may be partakers of the divine nature, having escaped the corruption that is in the world through lust. ~ 2 Pet. 1:3-4

24. God has given us abundance of grace and the gift of righteousness.

> For if by one man's offence death reigned through the one, much more those who receive abundance of grace and of the gift of righteousness will reign in life through the One, Jesus Christ ~ Rom 5:17

You can reign in life through Christ Jesus independent of circumstances.

You can reign in life because God has given you the gift of righteousness (right-standing with God) and abundance of grace (divine favor). We have access to this grace by faith. God's grace super abounds to us through His Word and the Holy Spirit.

25. God is perfect, exceedingly excellent.

God is perfect, exceedingly excellent, intrinsically

good and benevolent. W.E. Vine says, "God is essentially, absolutely and consummately good." There is no bad in His nature or His acts.

God is awesome in splendor, pure, holy, righteous, glorious, brilliant, magnificent, and beautiful beyond description. Heaven stands in awe of Him. Day and night, the living creatures cry, "Holy, Holy, Holy is the Lord God Almighty, Who was and is and is to come" (Rev 4:8).

26. God is forever faithful.

God is forever faithful, reliable, trustworthy, and true to His Word. God's faithfulness is because of who He is. All His promises are backed by all the honor of His Name. He will not break His covenant or ever altar His Word. (Ps 138:2; 89:34) Most certainly, if God said it, you can count on it.

27. God loves us. Nothing can separate us from His love.

The central truth underlying all that God does is the fact that "...God is Love" (1 Jn 4:8). He loves us and nothing can separate us from His love.

How great is the pure, selfless, merciful, unconditional agape love the Father has lavished on us, that we should be called children of God. (1 Jn 3:1) God's will for us is infinitely beyond all that we could ask or think. His will is nestled within His great love for us. God's love is perpetual. God's love never fails! (1 Cor 13:8)

> For I am persuaded that neither death nor life, nor angels nor principalities nor powers, nor things present nor things to come, nor height nor depth, nor any other created thing, shall be able to separate us from the love of God which is in Christ Jesus our Lord ~ Rom 8:38-39

28. The Lord will never leave you nor forsake you.

You are never alone. The Lord is always with you just as He promised: "Lo, I am with you always, even to the end of the age" (Mt 28:20b).

The Lord will never forsake you. He will never abandon, desert, or leave you in the lurch or desperate situation. The Lord will never leave you down in a set of circumstances that are against you.

> For He Himself has said, "I will never leave you nor forsake you" So we may boldly say, "The Lord is my helper; I will not fear. What can man do to me?" ~ Heb 13:5b-6

29. God will complete the good work He has begun in you.

> He who has begun a good work in you will complete it until the day of Jesus Christ. ~ Phil 1:6

30. Every adverse circumstance is temporary.

> While we do not look at the things which are seen, but at the things which are not seen. For the things which are seen are temporary, but the things which are not seen are eternal. ~ 2 Cor 4:18

Our life on earth is temporary. All life's circumstances are temporary. Every adverse circumstance can change in a moment, in the twinkling of an eye, in a nanosecond, by the supernatural intervention of God.

While, we may or may not receive an instant miracle (totally in God's discretion), we can rest assured that ultimately all things will work together for good to those who love God and are the called according to His purpose. (Rom 8:28)

31. The Lord is coming again.

> You also be patient. Establish your hearts, for the coming of the Lord is at hand. ~ Jas 5:8

***

You are a child of God on a sojourn in the earth. Your daddy is God Almighty, Creator of Heaven and earth and every living thing. You have a covenant of grace, love and peace with Him. Is anything too difficult for the Lord to do, or undo?

In light of these spiritual facts, we can live in victory every day no matter what is going on around us. We are not working to achieve victory. Christ is our victory. We have victory when we live, move, and have our being in Him. We can reign in life every day when we keep a heavenly point of view.

Key No. 10:

Rise Up, Declare and Decree Victory

Today is a new day. Endless possibilities and opportunities are before us. Let us rise up in the Spirit, confess, declare and decree victory. Let us release light and glory from Heaven into this day through a synergy of thanksgiving, praise, prayer, declarations, and decrees of faith based on God's Word.

Thanksgiving, Praise, Prayer, Declarations, Decrees

Father, thank you for this glorious day. This is the day that the Lord has made and I will rejoice and be glad in it. Lord, you are exceedingly great and exceedingly greatly to be praised. There is no one like you, nor is there any God besides you. Today my soul magnifies the Lord. My spirit rejoices in God my Savior. [Ps 118:24; Ps 145:3; Lk 1:46-47]

Thanks for redemption, forgiveness, the blood of Jesus

Father, thank you for redemption. Thank you for the gift of your son Jesus Christ. Thank you for the sinless blood of Jesus shed at Calvary, which blood was sprinkled on Heaven's mercy seat and accepted by you as payment in full for our sins forever.

Thank you for forgiving my sins and bringing me out of bondage.

Lord, thank you for redeeming me from the hand of the enemy. Thank you for redeeming my life from every distress. Thank you for redeeming my life from destruction. Thank you for the power of the blood of Jesus to stop plagues and neutralize any demonic attack against me.

[Eph 1:7; Ps 106:10; Ps 107:2; 1 Ki 1:29; Neh 1:10; Ps 103:4; Ex 12]

Thanks for the New Covenant

Thank you for the everlasting New Covenant, a covenant of great and precious promises, through which we may be partakers of the divine nature. [Mt 26:28; Heb 12:24; Heb 13:20; Heb 8:6; 2 Pet 1:4]

Rise Up, Declare and Decree Victory

Praise to Rock of Salvation

Lord, you are my Rock and my Fortress and my Deliverer in whom I trust. You are my Strength and Song and you have become my Salvation. You are my God and I will forever praise you. [Ps 18:2]

Bless the wonderful Name of Jesus (Yeshua)

Lord Jesus, your name is Wonderful. Your name is highly exalted above every name that is named, not only in this age but also in that which is to come.

Your name is above all principalities, powers, dominion, might, rule, government, and authorities. Your name is above every sickness and disease. At the name of Jesus every knee will bow and every tongue confess that Jesus Christ is Lord, to the glory of God the Father.

Lord, your name speaks total salvation and victory. While some trust in chariots, and some in horses, we will remember the name of the Lord our God. Lord, through your Name I have victory over all who rise up against me.

Oh Lord, our Lord, how excellent and glorious is your name in all the earth. Lord, you are worthy to receive glory, honor, majesty, praise, power, strength, and blessing. [Ps 20:7; Isa 9:6; Eph 1:21; Phil 2:9; Ps 8:9; Rev 4:11]

Thanks for fresh mercies, loving-kindness, faithfulness

Lord, thank you for your fresh and tender mercies that are over my life today. Thank you for your goodness and mercy that endure forever. Thank you for your loving kindness, which is better than life itself. Thank you for your faithfulness to all generations. Great is your faithfulness to me. [Lam 3:23; Ps 145:8-9; Ps 63:3; Ps 119:90; Ps 89:2]

Thanks for blessings, provision, and precious promises

Thank you for blessing me with all spiritual blessings in heavenly places in Christ Jesus. Thank you for giving me all things that pertain to life and godliness. Thank you that all the promises of God in Christ are *yes* and *amen* (so be it) to the glory of God. [Eph 1:3; 2 Pet 1:3; 2 Cor 1:20]

Thanks for the Holy Spirit

Thank you for the Holy Spirit, my Helper, Comforter, Counselor, Advocate, Standby, Intercessor, and Teacher who teaches me all things and reminds me of all things that you have said. [Jn 14:17; Jn 14:26; Jn 15:26]

Thanks for guidance

Father, thank you for your Word that continually guides me. Your Word is a lamp to my feet and a light to my path. Thank you that the Holy Spirit, the eternal Spirit of Truth, leads and guides me into all truth. [Isa 58:11; Ps 119:105; Jn 16:13]

Thanks for God's all-sufficient grace

Father, your Word says you are able to make all grace abound towards me so that I, always having all sufficiency in all things, may have abundance for every good work. Thank you for your all-sufficient grace. [2 Cor 9:8]

Thanks for God's love

Father, thank you for your amazing love for me. Thank you that nothing shall separate me from the love of God which is in Christ Jesus my Lord. [Rom 8:38-39]

Thanks for family and home

Lord, thank you for my family. Thank you for my children. Thank you for my home. Thank you for the blessings of food, clean water, shelter, clothing, strength and vitality.

Thanks for provision

Lord, thank you for meeting my needs according to your riches in glory by Christ Jesus. [Phil 4:19]

Thanks for protection

Lord, I am so thankful that you are my refuge and strength, my strong tower, my fortress. The righteous run into you and they are safe. Lord my soul trusts in you and under your wings I will take refuge. You are my refuge from the storms of life, my shade from the heat. [Ps 46:1; Ps 57:1; Ps 91:4; Isa 25:4]

Thanks for peace and joy

Father, thank you that I have peace with God and the supernatural peace of God. Divine peace controls my thoughts and emotions. Today I shall go out with joy and be led forth with peace. [Isa 32:17; Isa 54:10; Col 3:15; Isa 55:12]

Thanks for overcoming power

Father, thank you that I am born of God. That makes me an overcomer already. My faith in you is the victory that overcomes the world. I also overcome by the Blood of the Lamb and the word of my testimony. [Jn 1:13; 1 Jn 5:1; 1 Jn 5:4; Rev 12:11]

Thanks for victory in Christ

Thank you, Father, for always giving me the victory through my Lord Jesus Christ. Thank you that I can do all things through Christ who strengthens me. Thank you that I am more than a conqueror through Him who loves me. [1 Cor 15:57; Phil 4:13; Rom 8:37]

Authority to Bind and Loose

Lord, you have given us authority to bind and loose, to declare every spiritual activity either lawful or unlawful based on the revelation of your Word. [Mt 16:19; 18:18]

Loosing from works of the devil

Lord you have given us authority to tread on serpents and scorpions and over all the ability of the enemy. You have given us authority over principalities, powers, rulers of darkness and hosts of wickedness in the heavenly places. [Lk 10:19; Eph 1:21; 2:6]

Lord, right now I take authority over illegitimate spiritual activity in, over, and around my house. I declare the Blood of Jesus covers my house. I forbid the devil to operate in my household.

I declare my family loosed from fear, doubt, unbelief and confusion. We are loosed from every ungodly thought and attitude. We are loosed from every assignment, plan, plot, scheme, strategy and secret intent of the enemy.

I break the power of every ungodly word spoken over my life and over my household.

Binding to character and purposes of God

Lord, you are my complete armor. You are the truth. You are my righteousness. You are my Prince of Peace. You are my Savior. You are my shield of faith. You are the eternal Word of God. [Mt 18:18a; Jn 14:6; 1 Cor 1:30; Eph 6:10, 13-18; 1 Pet 1:23]

Lord, I declare that I am bound to You and your Word. I declare that my will activity wills to do the will of God.

Lord I bind myself and my household to your loving kindness and truth, which will lead and instruct our hearts. I bind myself and my family to your unconditional love which casts out fear. I declare that my family is knit together in the bonds of peace and love by the power of the Holy Spirit. [Prov 3:3-4; 1 Jn 4:18; Eph 4:3]

Declarations and Decrees

Lord, I declare that I will hear your voice and the voice of a stranger I will not heed nor follow. I will not turn to the right or to the left from your perfect path of peace and liberty. [Jn 10:4; Prov 3:17]

I will walk in the Spirit and not fulfill the lusts of the flesh. I will walk in divine truth and light. I will live by faith. I will walk in love. I will abide in you and allow your Word to abide in me. I will submit to your Word, your will and your way. [Gal 5:16; Rom 1:17; Jn 15:7]

I will bless you while I live; I will lift up my hands in your name. I will remember that it is you who gives me the power to get wealth that you may establish your covenant. [Jn 15:7; Ps 63:4; Deut 8:18]

I declare I am blessed going in and blessed coming out. Lord, I decree blessings over my family today. [Deut 28:6; Eph 1:3]

I decree that no sickness, disease, foul germ, bacteria or virus, pain or torment, can dwell in my body which is the temple of the Holy Spirit. I break the power of sickness and disease off my household. Lord, you are my refuge. I decree that no evil shall befall me and no plague shall come near my dwelling. [Ex 12:13; Ps 91:10]

I decree I will not slip, stumble or fall because you have given your angels charge over me to bear me up and keep me in all my ways lest I dash my foot against a stone. [Ps 91:11-12]

In the Name of Jesus I decree that no hurt, harm or calamity will befall me or my family.

I decree that no weapon formed against me shall prosper and every tongue that rises in critical judgment or condemnation against me shall be shown to be in the wrong, because you, Lord, are my righteousness. [Is 54:17; 1 Cor 1:30]

Lord, I decree that you are God over this nation. I decree that my neighborhood is blessed. My city is blessed. My state is blessed. My nation is blessed, in the Name of Jesus.

Exalt the Lord Most High

Be exalted O God, above the heavens. Be exalted among the nations. Be exalted in the earth. Let your glory be above all the earth. Let the whole earth be filled with your glory.

Yours, O Lord is the greatness, the power and the glory, the victory and the majesty; for all that is in heaven and in earth is yours. Yours is the kingdom, O Lord, and you are exalted as head over all. [Ps 46:10; 57:5; 72:19; 2 Chron 29:11]

Lord, I love You. I bless your glorious Holy Name today and forevermore. Amen and Amen.

Rejoice

Today, I laugh. I rejoice. In Christ Jesus I am empowered to prosper, empowered to overcome, empowered to reign victorious.

***

Notes

http://www.merriam-webster.com/dictionary

Nelson, Thomas C., New Spirit-Filled Life Bible (Nashville, Tn: Thomas Nelson Publishers, 2002)

Trench, R.C., Synonyms of the New Testament, Ninth Ed. 1880 (Grand Rapids, Michigan: Wm. B. Eerdman, 1947, reprint)

Vine, W.E., Expository Dictionary of Old and New Testament Words (Old Tappan, New Jersey: Fleming H. Revell Co., 1981)

Wuest, Word Studies in the Greek New Testament, Vol. 1 (Grand Rapids, Michigan: Wm. B. Eerdman, 1955)

Zodhiates, Spiro, Hebrew Greek Key Study Bible (Chattanooga, TN: AMG Publishers, 1991)

About the Author

CapazinThornton is a Bible teacher, speaker, and writer. She is the author of High Call to Pray, VICTORY 10 Keys for Living in Victory Every Day, and Keys for Powerful Intercessory Prayer. Capazin spends most of her time now writing and speaking. Capazin currently resides in south Orange County, California.

Connect with Capazin

website:	www.capazin.com
blog:	http://capazin.com/capazins-blog/
Facebook:	facebook.com/capazin.thornton

Resources by Capazin Thornton

You may order these and other resources through:

http://capazin.com

A uniquely powerful, concise practical guide to help believers develop a strong, Word based, Spirit led prayer life. You will learn many facets of prayer, prayer's true purpose, the character of God, the power of praying the Word, authority of the believer, the patience factor in prayer, dynamic expressions of praise, and how to pray Scripture based, Holy Spirit inspired prayers.

High Call to Pray
Paperback: $10:95 US
E-book: $5.99 US

www.ingramcontent.com/pod-product-compliance
Lightning Source LLC
LaVergne TN
LVHW052254070426
835507LV00035B/2899